I ALMOST GAVE UP

*Real pain. Real faith.
Real victory.*

COMPILED BY
DR. NATASHA BIBBINS

I Almost Gave Up © June 2025

Compiled by Dr. Natasha Bibbins

Published in the United States of America by

ChosenButterflyPublishing LLC

www.ChosenButterflyPublishing.com

All scripture quotations, unless otherwise indicated, are taken from the HOLY BIBLE, NEW INTERNATIONAL VERSION®. NIV® Copyright ©1973, 1978, 1984 by International Bible Society. Used by permission of Zondervan. All rights reserved.

Scriptures marked KJV are taken from the KING JAMES VERSION (KJV): KING JAMES VERSION, public domain.

Scriptures marked RSV are taken from the REVISED STANDARD VERSION (RSV): Scripture taken from the REVISED STANDARD VERSION, Grand Rapids: Zondervan, 1971

Scriptures marked NKJV are taken from the NEW KING JAMES VERSION (NKJV): Scripture taken from the NEW KING JAMES VERSION®. Copyright© 1982 by Thomas Nelson, Inc. Used by permission. All rights reserved.

Scriptures marked AMP are taken from the AMPLIFIED BIBLE (AMP): Scripture taken from the AMPLIFIED® BIBLE, Copyright © 1954, 1958, 1962, 1964, 1965, 1987 by the Lockman Foundation Used by Permission. (www.Lockman.org)

All rights reserved under International Copyright Law. Contents and/or cover may not be reproduced, distributed, or transmitted in any form or by any means or stored in a database or retrieval system, without the prior written consent of the publisher and/or authors.

ISBN: 978-1-945377-96-9
First Edition Printing
Printed in the United States of America

June 2025

TABLE OF CONTENTS

I Almost Gave Up: Visionary Preface	1
A Son's Testimony By William Battle	3
When God Steps In: A Testimony of Faith, Favor, and Protection By Naomi Prince	11
A Prophet Tears By Dr. Derrick R Zachary	21
Caged in Silence By Shana Turner	33
I Didn't Die There By Jaleesa Olds	43
Strengthened in the Struggle By Nicole Shrieves	55
Becoming By Carla D Manuel	67
Built to Survive, Called to Thrive By Tanikwa S. Matthews	87
Trust the Process By Teka Giddens	105
Delayed but Not Denied By Peri Hutt	125
The Edge of Giving up Is Where Breakthroughs Begin By Dr. Natasha Bibbins	145

I Almost Gave Up
Visionary Preface

There are moments in life when the weight of the world seems too heavy to bear, when the road ahead feels impossible, and when the temptation to quit becomes overpowering. I Almost Gave UpLike many of you, this was my story. For years, I wrestled with the idea of giving up, convinced that my dreams and aspirations were unattainable. I had moments of doubt, times when I thought I was destined to fail, times when I felt I had reached the end of my rope.

But life has a way of surprising you. Just when I thought I couldn't go on any longer, something unexpected happened. In the face of hardship, I found strength I didn't know I had, and in the midst of despair, I discovered hope. I realized that the greatest triumphs often come after the hardest struggles.

This book is a testament to the power of resilience, the beauty of persistence, and the undeniable truth that, sometimes, when you are almost ready to give up, you're on the brink of something amazing.

So, if you're holding this book in your hands, know that you're not alone. No matter where you are in your journey, this story is for you. Who would have thought? The greatest breakthroughs often come when you least expect them.

Throughout this journey, I learned that setbacks are not the end but rather the beginning of something new. Every failure, every setback, and every moment of uncertainty was simply life's way of preparing me for what was to come. In those dark moments, it was hard to see the light at the end of the tunnel, but now I can look back and understand that every challenge had a purpose, every detour led me closer to my true path. If I had given up then, I would never have discovered the incredible things that awaited me.

This book is not just a reflection of the authors' struggles but also a celebration of the lessons learned along the way. It's for anyone who has ever felt like giving up, for anyone who has ever questioned whether they are strong enough to keep going. Through the stories of others, I hope you'll find the courage to push forward, even when the world seems to be against you. Remember, you never know what's just around the corner—and sometimes the most remarkable chapters of our lives begin when we decide not to give up. Who would have thought?

Dr. Natasha Bibbins

A Son's Testimony
William Battle

"I know what it is to be in need, and I know what it is to have plenty. I have learned the secret of being content in any and every situation, whether well fed or hungry, whether living in plenty or in want. I can do all this through him who gives me strength." – Philippians 4:12-13.

Born in 1995 in Nassawadox, Virginia, I was raised by a single mother, Natasha Bibbins, and alongside my sister, Wilniqua Battle, in a small town. Growing up, life felt simple, even though challenges were always present. With a close-knit family, I believed the world was full of possibilities, and I was always convinced that I had a plan for the future. But when plan A failed, the clarity they once had quickly vanished. In those early years, the idea of "being a man" was shaped by the streets. The idea of power, respect, and reputation seemed to lie in running with the wrong crowd and becoming someone known to have influence. I didn't realize then that this pursuit would lead to self-doubt, destruction, and a painful wake-up call for me and my family.

Although I always possessed the natural traits of a leader, I was hesitant to embrace this role. The fear of disagreement and losing friends made it easier to follow others, to blend in rather than stand out. That path seemed easier for a time, but the internal struggle of following instead of leading weighed heavily. Life took a turn when I realized that the streets weren't the answer. This was where the real journey began—finding the strength to lead on my own terms and understanding that true strength lies in honesty, resilience, and learning to own up to my choices. Now I'm using the lessons learned from the missteps of the past to create a future that reflects the person I've become. No matter what, I still never gave up, although I sometimes came close.

The Journey to Change

The journey from feeling lost to finding purpose after leading instead of following has been challenging but rewarding. Through it all, I've learned that life's real power doesn't come from external validation but from the internal strength to rise, make choices, and stay true to yourself. Although my mom wasn't always in church, she ensured faith was present in our home. She played church music to get us in the spirit, creating an atmosphere of quiet reverence and spiritual grounding, even if we weren't physically attending church. Through these moments—those songs, those small acts—I began to understand the power of faith. It wasn't always about being in church but about carrying God's presence with you wherever you went.

As I navigated the temptations of youth and the confusion of not knowing where to go, faith became the anchor that kept me grounded. I realized that the strength to keep going, to lead instead of follow, came not from external validation or the streets but from the belief that you could overcome anything with God by your side. It was through this realization that I began to turn my life around. My story is one of redemption and growth, using the lessons learned from the struggles and the faith that guided me. I've learned that giving up is easy when you don't have God on your side, but with faith, there's always a way forward. And that's the message I want to share—to show others that no matter how hard life gets, FAITH can be the light that leads you through the darkness. So many times, I wanted to call it quits, but I didn't. Who would have thought I would still be here in a different mindset? I have a mindset to serve God. I am not perfect, but I am still striving. Who would have thought that those prayers that my mother and grandmother prayed would be the reason why I was covered in Blood?

As you read this book, please remember that your life may be rough now, but it's not the end. If you give up, you will never get to have what God has for you. Even if you come close to giving up, your testimony is right around the corner. You will then have a story and bear witness to someone "Who Would Have Thought that I would have survived all that I have gone through!

A Note to My Son:

A Mother's Love: A Picture I will NEVER Forget

The night I ALMOST lost you was a night I will never forget. While lying in my comfortable bed, wondering when you were coming home, suddenly a call came across to your pop's (what you call him), Michael Bibbins's phone. Because it was almost 11:00 p.m., we were trying to figure out why your sister was calling so late. When your pops said, "Hello," all we could hear was a scream—"Tookie just got shot!" What? How? Huh?

How could something like this happen to my baby? I could not understand. We then hunted to find you because we didn't get any information. No matter what, I didn't give up. We went to a hospital; you were not there. We went to another one and were told that you were there. Through it all, I still could not cry. All I could say was, "God, please let me see my baby!" I was still denied entry to see you when I finally found you. Very anxious, I kept peeping through the door to see if I could see you, but I couldn't.

After waiting for a couple of hours the surgeon finally called my name and we went to the back, not to see you but we went into a conference room—only to hear these words: "I need to be honest with you, you son is hurt bad and it's not looking good." She went on to say, "I don't believe he's going to make it!"

At this point, I was numb. I didn't know what to feel or how to feel. I only had one request: "Can I see my baby?"

"Yes," she said, "but be prepared."

Nearly passing out, I managed to make it to your room, and I saw you lying there, lifeless. I grabbed your hands and said, "Mommy is here." All I could think about was you being left in your car to die after someone tried to take your life for no reason at all. I looked at you and then looked up to God and said, "God, I forgive the young man who did this to my baby," with tears running down my face and still in disbelief that this could happen. I still had FAITH.

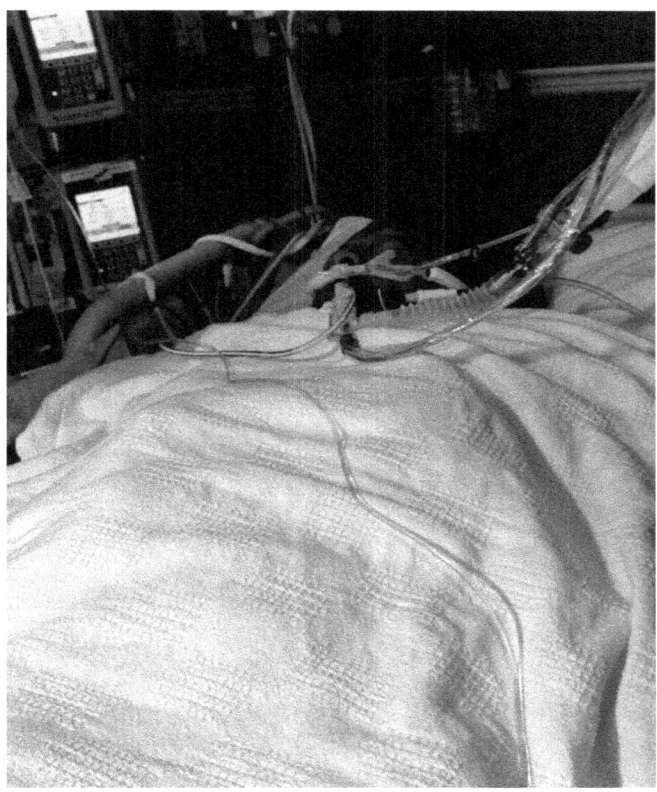

About four hours later, we met the Head Surgeon, who wanted me to know that they had to get you under surgery right away. He said, "I will do my best, but I don't think he will make it out."

I was able to walk down to the operating room with you. The surgeon asked, "Do you want one last kiss?"

I said, "I will give him one last kiss before he goes into surgery, BUT I will kiss my baby when he comes out of surgery!" I reached into my purse and grabbed my oil and sent you into surgery with a cross on your forehead, made with Holy Oil. I anointed your forehead, your hands, and your feet. I said, "Lord, I trust you!"

After waiting for hours for you to come out of surgery, my phone rang, and it was the head surgeon. Sounding relieved, he said, "I'm PLEASED, and he should completely recover."

NOBODY BUT GOD COULD HAVE DONE THIS. You see, Son, I could have accepted the surgeon's report; this is their specialty. But I know a man who's greater. I never gave up; I kept the FAITH and kept praying because the Bible declares in John 16:33, "I have told you these things, so that in me you may have peace. ***In this world, you will have trouble.*** But take heart. I have overcome the world."

Who would have thought you would still be here to share your journey?

WILLIAM'S ACKNOWLEDGEMENTS:

I want to thank my mommy, Natasha Bibbins, for everything. When I was wrong, you prayed for me. When I am doing right, you encourage me to keep going. I love you. I want to thank my Pops, Michael Bibbins. When I couldn't do for myself, you gave up your day to help me! I can never repay you for all you've done for me. I want to thank my sister, Wilniqua Battle – you already know, it's always been us! I love you, Sis. I am thankful for my grandma, Pastor Reid, who loves me unconditionally. Thank you!

To all my family and friends, I may not be able to name you one by one, but you already know what you mean to me. Jesse, Thomas, & Cameron, you already know. I love you all!

William Battle

William Battle, born Willie James White III, was born on the Eastern Shore of Virginia to his mother, Natasha (Walker) Bibbins, and father, Willie White Jr, in August 1995. William loved playing sports, especially basketball. He graduated from Nandua High School while living on the Eastern Shore with his grandmother, Pastor Hattie Reid, and grandfather, Deacon Charlie Reid.

William graduated from Merchant Marine School in 2024, with hopes of leaving Virginia to start a better life for himself. Although life took a different course, the dream remains alive.

William has many siblings, and he loves them all, but there's one who's always been by his side, and that's Wilniqua Battle. He has also been blessed to have a "bonus father," Michael Bibbins, who loves him as if he were his own.

On December 14, 2002, William lost his favorite uncle, Leotoles (Leotis) Reid, in a traffic accident. This shattered his heart.

When God Steps In: A Testimony of Faith, Favor, and Protection

Naomi Prince

I will be sharing one of the most challenging yet faith-affirming moments of my life—a time when I almost gave up but discovered God's hand powerfully at work. Through an ectopic pregnancy that threatened my life and the life of my unborn child, I experienced God's protection, grace, and favor. This chapter is a testament to the fact that God's plans for us transcend the storms we face. It's a journey of faith, trust, and surrender, where His promises prevail even in the most unimaginable circumstances.

When Life Took an Unexpected Turn

In April 2013, I discovered I was pregnant and it felt like a fresh wave of hope and joy entered my life. The thought of bringing a new life into the world filled me with so much anticipation. I began imagining what the months ahead would hold—prenatal appointments, baby shopping, and the eventual joy of holding my child in my arms.

At around four weeks pregnant, everything seemed perfectly normal. My body was adjusting and I had no reason to believe this pregnancy would be anything other than smooth. However, that peace was short-lived. It began with mild discomfort that soon escalated into sharp abdominal pain. At first, I tried to brush it off as typical pregnancy symptoms, but the intensity of the pain forced me to seek medical attention.

When I arrived at the hospital, the doctors ran a series of tests, including ultrasounds and bloodwork. After hours of waiting anxiously, they told me I had a ruptured cyst that had caused blood to leak into my abdomen. They assured me that it would resolve on its own and admitted me to monitor my condition for a couple of days. During my stay, I was hopeful. The doctors' reassurances made me believe this was just a small bump in the road.

After being discharged, I returned home, determined to rest and take care of myself. However, just two weeks later, the pain returned with a vengeance.

The Diagnosis No One Wants to Hear

I still vividly remember that morning. It was around 5:00 a.m. and, as was my routine, I joined our daily prayer call. I valued this time of prayer and fellowship with the intercessors, but that morning, something felt different. As I prayed, I felt the same pain from before, but this time, it was much more intense. The sharpness of it made me stop mid-prayer.

Before ending the call, I asked the intercessors to pray for me, even though I couldn't fully articulate what I was feeling. I just knew I needed their prayers. By the time the call ended at 5:30 a.m., the pain had worsened to the point where I could barely move. I was on the couch in my living room and even shifting slightly felt unbearable.

As a family childcare provider, I had children arriving early in the morning, but by God's grace, they were all still asleep. I struggled to manage the basics that morning, calling out to my husband for help. Even with his assistance, I couldn't stand and I knew this wasn't something I could ignore.

We called 911 and while waiting for the ambulance I began arranging for the children in my care to be taken to another provider. The parents of the children were incredibly understanding and one even offered to help transport them. My husband ensured our school-aged children made it to the bus stop before he followed the ambulance to the hospital.

The ride to the hospital was excruciating. Every bump on the road felt like it was amplified tenfold. When I finally arrived, the medical team quickly got to work. They ordered a sonogram, took blood samples, and checked my vitals. I could sense from their faces that something wasn't right and, soon enough, they delivered devastating news: I had an ectopic pregnancy.

The baby had implanted in my fallopian tube, which had expanded dangerously and was leaking blood into my abdomen. The doctors informed me that immediate emergency surgery was necessary to save my life. As if that news wasn't overwhelming enough, they delivered another shocking revelation: I was still pregnant. Another baby was growing in my womb.

The Crossroads of Faith

I was left alone in the hospital room, trying to process the whirlwind of emotions and information. My husband had to return home to pick up our youngest child from the bus stop, leaving me in a space where it was just me and God.

Questions flooded my mind. Why was this happening? Why didn't they catch this earlier? How could I have both an ectopic pregnancy and another baby in the womb? My heart was heavy and fear threatened to overtake me.

In the middle of my questioning, I picked up the phone and called my husband, my mom, and the intercessors. I needed their prayers. The intercessors began praying fervently and their words reminded me that I wasn't alone in this battle.

As the medical team prepared me for surgery, I felt a quiet nudge in my spirit. It was as though God was asking me to make a decision: Would I let fear control me or would I choose to trust Him completely?

I chose to trust Him.

God's Peace in the Operating Room

The moments leading up to the surgery were surreal. As they wheeled me into the operating room, I whispered prayers to God, reminding Him of His promises. Despite the chaos around me, I felt His peace wrap around me like a warm blanket.

I remember the medical staff telling me they were about to administer the anesthesia and as they counted backward, I silently declared, "God, I trust You."

The surgery was a success. The doctors removed the ectopic pregnancy and, miraculously, my fallopian tube hadn't ruptured despite being severely swollen. They later described it as a hot dog that had been overcooked, ready to burst. The fact that it hadn't ruptured was nothing short of a miracle.

However, the ordeal wasn't over. I had lost a significant amount of blood during the procedure and my levels were dangerously low. The doctors warned that I might need a transfusion if my levels didn't improve.

I prayed again, asking God to restore my body. I declared healing over myself, believing that He could regulate my blood levels. By the next morning, my levels had begun to rise steadily and the doctors confirmed that I wouldn't need a transfusion.

A Living Testimony

The next hurdle was determining if the baby in my womb had survived. The medical team was doubtful, given the trauma my body had endured, but I reminded God of His Word and prayed fervently.

The ultrasound technician prepped me for the scan and began the process in silence. The room felt still and time seemed to stretch endlessly. I prayed quietly and then I heard God speak clearly: "Trust Me." Finally, the technician broke the silence and asked, "Would you like to see your baby?" My heart leapt with joy as she turned the screen toward me. There on the screen was my baby, alive and thriving. The sight brought tears to my eyes and I felt an overwhelming sense of gratitude.

In that moment, God spoke again, saying, "Do you see how the baby is protected in this sac? Just as this baby is shielded from everything going on around it, so I protect My children."

Covered by His Grace

As I reflected on everything that had happened I was reminded of a prayer spoken over me the day before the surgery. I had attended church for the first time in weeks and brought a bottle of anointing oil to be prayed over. During the service, my pastors laid hands on my belly and declared, "The baby is covered in the blood of Jesus and all is well concerning this child."

God had already gone ahead of me, preparing the way for what I didn't know was coming. That prayer became a cornerstone of my faith during this trial, reminding me that God is always in control.

Conclusion: Faith That Overcomes

Looking back on this journey, I am in awe of God's faithfulness. He showed me that, even in the most challenging moments, He is present, working behind the scenes for our good. I experienced both death and life at the same time—losing one child while another was being formed in my womb. And today, that child is alive and well, a living testament to God's divine plan.

This experience was never just about me. It was also about the life that needed to come forth, the purpose that had to be fulfilled, and the people God destined to be connected to this testimony. So often, we only see our struggles through the lens of how they affect us, but God's perspective is greater. Our trials are never just about what we endure—they are also about the lives that will be impacted because of our obedience to keep moving forward.

This testimony is a reminder that, no matter what storms we face, God's plans for us are always good. He is our protector, healer, and peace in the midst of chaos. Even in loss, He births new purpose. Even in sorrow, He brings forth joy. Trust Him and He will carry you through every trial, turning your pain into purpose and your struggles into a testimony of His unfailing grace.

Naomi's Acknowledgments:

First and foremost, I give all glory and honor to God, who has proven time and time again that He is a faithful and loving Father. Without His strength, grace, and favor, I would not be here to share this testimony.

To my husband, your unwavering love and support during this time meant everything to me. You were my rock when I felt like I was crumbling. To my children, you are constant reminders of God's blessings in my life.

To my parents, church family at the time, and the intercessors who labored in prayer on my behalf, thank you for standing in the gap and believing God for my healing and restoration. Your prayers were instrumental in this journey.

Finally, to every reader, my prayer is that this story reminds you that even when you feel alone, God is right there with you. May your faith be strengthened as you read of His faithfulness

Naomi Prince

Naomi Prince is the mouthpiece of God, a wife, a mother, and a business owner. She is called to declare and teach the unadulterated Word of God, pointing everyone she encounters back to God and the mandate of kingdom building and winning lost souls. She fulfills this calling by encouraging others in the art of applying God's Word in prayer and obeying His instructions. Naomi is a proud member of Spirit of Glory Worship Center under the leadership of Apostle John & Pastor Talein Harris. She firmly believes that every person born on the earth has a God-ordained assignment and passionately desires to see them fulfill it.

Naomi is a graduate of Liberty University, where she earned both an AA in Early Childhood Education and a BS in Elementary Education. As a Homeschooling Educator and Tutor, she is the founder and Business Owner of Kingdom United Solutions, LLC, where she specializes in helping families with individualized homeschooling and tutoring services.

She believes homeschooling is an opportunity to shape minds and hearts, encouraging parents and caregivers that they can educate their children effectively and efficiently.

In 2024, God birthed Kingdom Ignite Global Ministries through Naomi, establishing a global mandate to teach, disciple, and raise up individuals rooted in kingdom principles. Within this ministry, Naomi founded the Eight-Week Prayer Mentorship Program, Kingdom Ignite Prophetic Community, and Kingdom Ignite Mentorship Academy, all of which are designed to equip believers with the tools to fulfill their divine assignments. Through dynamic teaching, prayer mentorship, and discipleship, Naomi cultivates a thriving community focused on kingdom building and winning souls for Christ. Her heart's desire is to see lives transformed and aligned with God's purpose, empowering individuals to step boldly into their God-given destinies.

Contact Information

Organization: Kingdom United Solutions, LLC | Kingdom Ignite Global Ministries **Email:** naomiprince@kingdomunitedsol.com

Website: www.kingdomunitedsol.com

Social Media Handles:

Facebook: https://www.facebook.com/millerprince

https://www.facebook.com/p/Kingdom-United-Solutions-100063019880704/

Instagram: @naomiprince07 | @kingdomunitedsolutions

A Prophet Tears
Dr. Derrick R Zachary

Who would have thought that I would be on a path that God had handpicked for me to be? A voice in the wilderness, a voice to the people, and a voice to bring people of out an Egypt mentality. It is always easy to talk about the goodness of the Lord, but few ever discuss the hardship that comes with been chosen. The only way to help you understand this journey is to share mine with you.

The journey starts with the birthing process. The moment when the enemy desires to take you out before you are born. What did I just say? Yes, before I was born there was a snake that crawled on my mother's belly when she was eight months pregnant with me. The very next month, month nine, meaning birth and the fruit of the Spirit, I was born in Opelousas, LA, which I was not supposed to be at, but I was coming. There was no doctor on the scene, just a nurse, and my beautiful head of hair was out and my head crying as my mother put it. The nurse did not know what to do, but my mother said, "You better catch this baby." September 23, 1975, I made a miraculous entrance.

Accept yourself for who you are, always stand out. It's going to come with trials; it's going to come with tribulation, but you are equipped to handle the storm and different weathers, you have nothing to prove to anyone. Go hard and be strong, the world depends on you. It sounded good to say, but I'm reminded of all of the assaults, molestation and abuse that I endured before I got to be a teenager. It all started at three years old when I was taken into a chicken coop and was forced to have sex with a cousin. My life began to trickle down and heal from there as being second to the oldest I never fitted in with the older siblings or the younger siblings—I was the in between. Protecting everyone while no one was protecting me. I would wake up in the middle of the night to hands playing with my private parts and having to fight cousins.

At five years old I was at my older brother's birthday celebration outside in the yard having a tent sleepover. Being the youngest in the tent they played a game of truth in there and they dared a 13-year-old to have sex with me. I was crying saying, "I'm not going to do this," but the only way that I could get out of it was to take a beating from everybody in the tent. I thought my brother was going to protect me, but he just watched it happen to me. From that moment on I simply hated anything that resembled people. Still, with all that going on and enduring day after day, as it would seem to me, I kept protecting other people, fighting for other people—but still nobody was protecting me!

What I needed in my life was real love from everyone. Through different trials I was growing up too fast and didn't have time to enjoy being a child. Going through being looked over for holidays and birthdays. Just different events made me feel that I was unwanted or I wasn't good enough. I also needed the protection from family to make sure that I was safe. All the things that I experienced as a child made me harder, made me curious, made me feel like I didn't know my place and what I could offer people besides my body.

I talked to God so much; I just thought He'd never heard me, which made me even angrier towards everyone. Fighting was such a part of my life that being willing to do harm to anyone came so naturally. You never know what you create when you mishandle God's chosen. However, at the mention of Jesus' name I can remember sitting in the church and just would cry. I could hear him, feel him, and see him but never understood it. I grew up Catholic and Baptist—now figure that out.

Age 13–16- This life I hated it the most! My mother had gotten remarried to my stepfather who was 10 years older than I was. I started developing fast and everyone wanted a piece. My mother tried to take her own life. By the grace of God the state did not take us away from her because she was battling with her own issues after my father passed. I would break up relationships just because I could. I made up my mind that if I wasn't happy no one would be happy.

I also came to Christ around this time frame because I was tired. I received salvation at 14 and was filled with the Holy Ghost in the same week and I also was going to be adopted by the pastors of the church. Every pastor and prophet would always tell my mother, "You love all your kids except for one."

Her response to me or to them would be, "He just wants attention," which was something I had never received and didn't know what it looked like and I was full of anger, so much so that I planned to kill my entire family. I plotted their murder; I was going to stab all of them! My heart was hurting bad and nobody understood or cared.

Age 17–19- Around this time, I was going to drop out of school because I was having a hard time. However, I endured to make sure that I graduated. I was the first in my family to graduate high school as all the rest of my siblings dropped out. I also got accepted into college and I remember being dropped off by a white lady whose son I was teaching gymnastics to. I learned how to do praise dance at the age of 17. I did my first performance in downtown Atlanta in front of 27,000 people for the March of Jesus; imagine the one no one showed up for was before thousands to do something that gave me joy. I also had to speak to the youth about taking a stand for Christ.

Age 20–24- This season saw a shift in my entire life. I was living off campus for college and was visiting a store where I was sexually assaulted by a white man who was married, which shaped my entire life once again. I ran up to the school to find my best friend and told her what was going on. I was crying profusely and called my mother and told her I was coming home to talk to her. When I got there, she looked me in my face and said, "If you were my daughter I would do something about it; but maybe you wanted this to happen." My heart fell to the ground. My friends looked at me and said, "Did your mama just blow you off like you don't mean anything?"

I spoke to many people in the church about what I was feeling and every time I reached out, they would turn around and say, "I've been waiting on you because I always wanted you." I would stay at preachers' houses and they would come into the room and jump on me and insert my penis inside of them. I would get a hard-on for some strange reason, which always bothered me. I never understood why someone would get a hard-on while people are trying to sexually assault them. Here I go blaming myself; maybe I wanted it to happen to me.

Around this time, I got into stripping in a club even though I hated showing my body. I liked the thrill of knowing that I could lure you in. I would just sleep around with everyone. I didn't care; I didn't want to live. I slept with people who I knew were HIV positive, had AIDS, had other things. I did not want to live at all.

January of 2000, I found out that I was HIV positive and also found out that he had a child and I was broken. I was going to take my life; I had made up in my mind I was going to die anyway the men in my family never live long so I was one of those ones that was not going to live long. This baby was in my arm, and I said if I don't live for anyone else, I will live for him. So, my son William is who made me live in spite of all of the stuff I was enduring just to try to fit in.

The whole while being in Atlanta I was just a pawn that people would use to advance their church status or their careers. I asked the Lord to take me out of Georgia, take me anywhere. Immediately my job asked me to go train people in their store in Washington, DC. It's where God started really dealing with me about my life. While in DC I got involved in a church in Maryland. They knew the prophetic on my life and the giftings. I met a young lady there; we ended up getting engaged and were planning to get married in 2007. Two weeks before the wedding, I called it off because she was tripping and I let her trip right on out the door. In that same year, September, I ended up having a slight heart attack a week before my birthday. I was upset with the Church and the Lord.

Haven't I endured enough! The Lord told me I was coming back to Atlanta; I told him I refused to go back. "I'm not going back."

The Lord spoke to me and said, "There are people that are waiting on you."

My response was, "I don't care. Let them wait!"

While in DC the Lord gave me a church name, Walking in Authority International Ministries. I told him, "I don't know why you giving me a name of a church because I am not opening one up."

There were so many days of crying, so many days of feeling like a failure, so many days of wondering why God put me in these circumstances. Who would have thought that I would still be preaching, prophesying, pastoring, dancing, singing, etc. for God? Can you even imagine being blamed for raping someone? Well, me neither!

There are many days of loneliness, there are many days of "I don't think I can do it," and there are many days of "How many more people can I help or inspire to become who God has created them to be?" It also still comes with rejection, hurt, disappointments, and lies. But one thing that the Lord has taught me is the word altar: apply love to all relationships.

This is what the Lord said to me:

"My life application is my mind becomes your mind. My body becomes your body. My wisdom becomes your wisdom. My wind becomes your wind. My thoughts become your thoughts. For I have made you of a new kind of people that shall invoke my presence. Do not fear for this shall be strange to you but not strange to me. For you shall walk in places where your feet shall never touch the ground and I will take you into the deepest part of me that you have not experienced. There's much to like for I will stretch you in my dimensional place, I have unlocked my hidden codes to propel my people out of the dark places. This shall be new to you, but your oil will remain in operation for it shall fill barrels that you have not seen. You will cause wells to spring up in desolated places for this is my word to you," says the Lord.

"How much you have access to the deepest part of me that will transcend dimensional portals. You have captivated my heart and the cherubim and seraphim are bringing everything you need. You shall go and recover all. Nothing shall have access to you but me," says the Lord. "I cause my wind to bring you new minerals. I have canceled all distractions for you. You shall be the chain reaction in the land for the world will seek for answers and it shall be found in you to provide clarity of my next move. They will seek you out, it is my will. I will cause my words to work for you because you possess my spirit. Now stampede through the land for it is yours to subdue and overtake," says the spirit of the Lord.

Who would have thought that this would be my legacy. No matter what, God gets all the glory. Never allow your circumstances and what you've been through to dictate what you are destined to be. God has a purpose for you and everything becomes a testimony that He is a sovereign God that can pull you out of anything.

That is the life of a prophet. Are you truly willing to go through the journey?

Apostle Derrick Zachary

Apostle Derrick Zachary is the founder of Walking in Authority International Ministries and Walking in Authority International Fellowship of Churches. He was born in Opelousas, LA and currently resides in Atlanta, GA. As a young man he never knew the purpose of his life, but he did know that God had a plan for him and that it was going to be great.

Apostle Zachary attended college in Toccoa, GA, where he studied music and communications.

He has been in ministry for more than 27 years. His first speaking engagement was done at the age of 17, in front of 27,000 people, in downtown Atlanta, for the March for Jesus.

He is noted for being one of the first men in Atlanta to perform Praise Dance and Mime. God used that as a platform to get him through many doors that led to numerous souls being healed, delivered, and set free. Apostle Zachary has been used in many capacities that include but are not limited to helping set up churches.

Presently, Apostle Zachary has a degree in the field of Medical Assistance and Healthcare Management, just recently receiving an Honorary Doctor of Divinity from the School of the Great Commission in South Carolina. He says he always has this scripture in mind: "Cry loud and spare not tell my people about their sins." Isaiah 58:1. He considers himself just another soldier down in the trenches like everyone else. He has assisted in building up many ministries, setting a foundation of order and training for those to know where they fit in the kingdom.

Apostle Zachary wrote his first book this year titled *Psalms of a Prophet; In the Midst of It All I Got an Answer*, which is available on Amazon and Kindle. He has also created a scholarship on Bold.org that is given out to students young and older twice a year.

Apostle Zachary has also started moving forward in the music and the movie world that God has set before him. He has done a stage play, "Safe Place," which deals with AIDS/HIV Awareness, with KPO Productions. He did his first web series titled "You Stand; We Stand

Together" directed by Charay Vaughn. He was quoted as saying, "I could not escape what God had for me. I am reminded that many are called but few are chosen. God uses me to restore the churches back to where they need to be by speaking out against sin and giving depth, insight and revelation to God's Word." He is known as the Great Illustrator.

During this season Apostle Derrick Zachary is bringing together organizations from around the world and teaching all denominations that we must come together as one body in Christ. He leaves us with this statement: "As my overseer, Apostle LaDonna Akowonjo of Full Gospel International, says, I was born to worship." They presently have a church that they are building up, located in Nigeria, Africa. In this time of teaching the altar, Apply Love To All Relationships is the platform that we continue to stand on.

Dr. Derrick R Zachary LLC

email: derrickrzachary@yahoo.com

Facebook: Derrick Zachary

Instagram: Dr.DZachary

http://walkinginauthourity-intl.webs.com/

CAGED IN SILENCE
Shana Turner

As a little child, I witnessed so many things. Although my mother and father tried to shelter me, it was hard not to see. I remember when my sperm donor used to come into the house drunk and beat my mother and I would be screaming for him to stop as a helpless three-year-old who could not help my mother. I watched and could hear the many nights of turmoil that my beautiful mother endured. I can see the little white house so vividly, even now as an adult. I remember my mother fighting back and running out of the house to escape to my grandmother's house, which was in the same yard. I couldn't understand why this man would allow himself to hurt such a beautiful soul. What could she possibly have done so wrong? How could he do this to his family? Then came two more babies that my grandmother would deliver as a midwife. I had two brothers years later and I wondered, *Could this be the beginning of my sperm donor changing? My mother is safe now from him, simply because she is pregnant.* This was love, or so I thought, normalizing that this is how a man and woman interact. You make up and everything goes away. The crazy thing is years went by and this man, whom I somehow admired and loved, decided after all the agony he created in our lives to leave us! I remember him telling me he would be back, but he never returned. I watched my mother, as a single mother of three, survive to take care of her family. We grew up with not much, but I appreciated the struggle later in life. If the world shut down today, I would know how to survive as an ESVA girl. I was quiet, shy and confused.

Later in life, things began to change for my family; my mother met a man, whom I called my father, and he became the provider to our extended family. I really wasn't sure of him at first, just due to all the hurt and abandonment I endured as a child. I didn't want my mother to get hurt again. I felt as the oldest that I needed to be the protector. We gave him hell, but he didn't give up on us. We didn't have much but made the best of it. My sperm donor never returned to check on us or give any financial support. I grew a dislike for him in silence. I blamed him for all the situations we endured and couldn't understand how he could do this to us.

Even though I was angry with him, he eventually came from out of nowhere and wanted to see us; my brothers were not feeling it, but I desired to see him. I was hoping that going on a trip with him to where he lived at the time would make me feel better—after all, I came from his DNA. Well, that wasn't what I thought it was. He took me to where he had made his new family and introduced me to a sister; I cannot recall her name, but this was painful to me as a child. How could he have another child? I observed that he was kind and gentle to his new family but gave us hell. I bottled all of this up and just took it as if I was spending time with him. A child wants and desires to be loved; I wanted to belong and feel that I was loved. After all, this was supposed to be my father! Regardless of the abuse, it's strange that after watching so many negatives from this man, I still wanted to be near him.

I look at my life now and understand why I made poor choices in men. We don't realize that childhood trauma affects us, we make poor decisions due to this. Parents are supposed to be our protectors, but no one taught them how to be a parent. We learn to live in silence and sweep it under the rug and countless episodes from childhood trickle into adulthood. There are so many life events that occurred for me as a child, too many to speak about, but it all started with my abusive father.

Cards Dealt

Moving forward from childhood into *"adulting."* I became a mother for the first time. I had a son and he was my everything. I wasn't seasoned in relationships, so I gave my virginity to my son's father. I was excited to have a relationship but not knowing that the ship was sailing all around me and making stops. I became a mother at the age of 19. When you think that the person you're with is your everything and that you will be the best parent in the world, it all seems so great at the time. You say, "I'm definitely going to do it differently than my parents." I learned a valuable lesson: things are not always what they seem. I was left with taking care of my son alone, due to the father tapping out and coming in and out of my life when he chose to. I was in love, or so I thought!

I continued to stay in and out of a toxic, unhealthy relationship, all because I didn't want to fail and have my son without his foundation. I won't go into the details of what transpired, but let's just say I was a fool and should have got off the ship a long time ago. I had a great support system from my family and his, but my son needed more than that. I always wanted more and was a dreamer, which in today's world we call manifesting.

I decided that I wanted to turn my gift of doing hair into a legitimate status, so I left and went to hair school. One of the hardest decisions I could ever have made was to leave my baby and head to school. I didn't trust people too well, especially being a victim of childhood sexual abuse. I remember the day I left to attend school; one of my mother's friends said that I could live with her. I attended school and would walk every day to class and it was not in a great neighborhood. I just wanted to make it and be great.

I met this young man who lived in the neighborhood; he was charming so we became friends and eventually dated. Well, this was strike two in my life. He turned out to be controlling and obsessive; that's when I learned about dating abuse. Remember I was the silent one. No one knew that I was going through this and no matter how I tried to break it off he wouldn't let go. In addition to this, where I resided with my mom's friend her boyfriend would continue to make sexual passes at me—here I am again being silent because it was the only place I could stay. I finally had a conversation with the other female roommate and found out she was going through the same thing, so we both agreed to tell my mom's friend. I ended up leaving and getting a place with a friend from my class's sister.

Here we go again, strike three. First apartment with a deranged roommate—big mistake. If you're old enough to remember the movie *Single White Female* times 10. During this time, I met my daughter's father. A beautiful bundle of joy and a girl. I always said if I ever had children that I wanted a girl and a boy. Strike one again, single mom trying to make it for her family. I went back home and lived with my mother, trying to figure it out and continue in my trade. I was a success at my gift. A year later, after I'm minding my business and not caring about being in a relationship or with anyone else, I met my youngest son's father. I wasn't aware of who he was because I didn't go out much and was just focused on being a mother and how to excel. Strike two again; this came with a lot of drama, and I wasn't for it, so I removed myself from the situation. I was being harassed by his significant other and her friend telling me it's not his baby and I was a nobody. Here I am saying I had no knowledge of him being with anyone or about her, but they wouldn't let up.

I wasn't getting any financial support from dad 1 or dad 3. I didn't give up and continued to try to make things great for my family. The struggle was real, being a single mom with no support. I decided that I wasn't waiting on any system and opened my first business. My clientele was booming. Then comes the next charmer. I married this one without my family knowing right away. All I wanted was a family with a mother and father for my children; then came strike three again! I ended up being the provider for my whole family while he wouldn't hold a job.

I asked for his support since I was clothing and feeding the family, securing the roof over our heads, taking vacations, and transportation. Well, that didn't happen. He was a great babysitter when he wasn't taking my children to hang out with his groups to enjoy his life. He lied, cheated and then some. I decided that I needed to exit the marriage, and leave him, but he didn't make it easy for me. I moved to an area to excel and to have a better environment for my family. I wanted to be where I knew they would get the best education and safe environment. Somehow, I couldn't manage it all and ended up homeless. I asked my mother to take my children until I found another place. I ended up working in addition to doing hair but trying to maintain sending funds for my children and living in a hotel put me in a car sleeping. Another silent moment in my life. I couldn't stand the fact that I was away from my children and it was eating me up on the inside. I felt I was a failure and wanted to take my life one night in the hotel room. I called my mother and she prayed for me! After this I went hard, all I wanted was my children with me, so I fought the fight and remained humble through all my pain and disappointments. I continued to endure so many trials but never gave up. I take accountability for not knowing and allowing others into my life. I had many losses, too many to name. I have so much to tell but not enough time in this book.

The greatest loss in my life was losing my son, Shaquille T. Turner, to senseless gun violence at the age of 25. My life has not been the same and will never be. He was supposed to be able to come home and live his life to the fullest. We are not supposed to bury our children. Every day is like a movie, but I will continue to keep his legacy alive. I don't want my story to be your story, nor do I look for sympathy. I will continue to be the voice for all lives lost and for the families left behind. I hope and pray this story will be a blessing to someone, if not many. I am sharing a little snippet of myself. I share to enlighten and encourage. I am imperfect; this is not to belittle anyone in my past but to share my transparency. Through it all, I almost gave up, but who would have thought that I would be here today sharing my story with you.

Shana Turner

Shana Turner was born on September 14th, 1969, in a small town on the Eastern Shore of Virginia named Painter, VA. She graduated from TCC with her associate in social science and NSU to finish her bachelor's in nursing. Shana is the oldest of her siblings. She was raised by her mother and father, Sandra and James Brickhouse. Shana was raised during a time of poverty, but that gave her a mindset of wanting more. She comes from a family of scientists, entrepreneurs, educators, musicians, and city council members; therefore, her drive to succeed has always been impeccable.

Shana has owned many businesses and is not shy of driving her own career. She also has dedicated her time to many organizations, just to name a few: Relay for Life, Black Lives Matter, Susan G. Coleman, and suicide prevention walks; she has been a community advocate prior to the loss of Shaq.

Shana has since led her organization on many levels. For instance, Wear Orange, Advocacy Day, National Night Out, Survivors' Week, National Victims' Crime Week, March for Our Lives, State Neighborhood winner, assisting those in need, Walks, and many other preventative aspects. She has a heart that desires to help everyone and always provide support.

Shana has three children named Rakeem, Kiara, and Shaquille. She also has three grandchildren, their names are Xavier, Micah, and Journee. Shana raised her children as a single mother, trying to beat the odds of the statistical rates of a woman who raises children alone. She beat the odds again. She raised three beautiful children who are very successful in their lives. Shana built the American dream for her children alone and, despite every trial she encountered, she never gave up.

On December 12th of 2017, Shana's life came to a halt. She received a phone call saying that her youngest of three, Shaquille T. Turner, was gunned down on his way home from work. Shaquille's senseless death left his community in a state of confusion as he was an exceptional young man with a promising future and a great head on his shoulders. Shaquille shined his light and his sense of humor allowed him to reach all walks of life. In his honor, Shana founded HR MASK & JRMASK, our youth, to keep Shaquille's legacy alive and uplift families that are affected by senseless killings. HR MASK was set up to drive the voice of the innocent lives taken and touched. Its intentions are to amend intentional act laws, 911, HIPAA, Mental Health, re-entry patterned with

ODAR LLC, Issues, and a closer look into the NICS system and how violence has affected our underserved communities. HR MASK sets out to have communities involved with youth as well as having communities get together with public officials and law enforcement to buckle down on violence. HR MASK is here to spread awareness, educate, and, most importantly, to be the voice of all lives lost and the families left behind. Shana is also the Regional Lead of Virginia for VBMU, the Woodson Center, Violence Interrupter, Outreach for VOCCA, Virginia Medical Reserve, Ambassador of District 7, and many other accolades.

Social media:

Shana@hrmask.org book me to speak

hrmask@facebook,

instagram hrmask@tiktok

I Didn't Die There
Jaleesa Olds

Abusive Relationship, Arrested, Insecure, Depression, and Mourning, I almost gave up, but who would have thought I made it through. I always explain my college experience as going into a dark tunnel and eventually coming out on the other side. I went in that tunnel a young girl, not having a relationship with God, not knowing her worth, and came out a woman of God.

One of my favorite Bible verses is James 1:2–4 Consider it pure joy, my brothers and sisters, whenever you face trials of many kinds, because you know that the testing of your faith produces perseverance. Let perseverance finish its work so that you may be mature and complete not lacking anything. I went through many kinds of trials, some of them being my fault and others to mature me as a woman.

Consider it pure joy!

Freedom. That's the first word that most young adults think of when they leave for college. Freedom from their parents' rules; however, the freedom to do anything has consequences. After freshman year, I decided to get a boyfriend, although that went against my mother's will. What I thought might be me meeting my husband turned into a physically and emotionally abusive relationship. My mother once told me one of my cousins was going through an abusive relationship and I remember saying, "That will never happen to me." Never say never!

At first it was like a fairy tale; flowers, dates, endless conversations. Then, over time, he would pick with me or talk down to me. My friends could see the difference in me when I talked to him or was around him because he had control over me. I remember one night I had given him a necklace and then we started arguing outside. As we were arguing he called out my name and I snatched the necklace off. When I did, he slapped me so hard my nose started to bleed and I fell to the ground. In that moment I grabbed the dirt and didn't want to live anymore. The physical and verbal abuse had me so low and ashamed. How could I let this happen to me when I come from a good family, beautiful and smart? But what I thought was love wouldn't let me leave him.

However, in this bad relationship, I experienced God for the first time. One night, at my apartment, he had me crying in a corner. I remember a tangible peace coming over me and letting me know everything would be alright. I stopped crying because the Holy Spirit, the comforter, came to let me know I would make it through!

During this time, I was going to church sometimes. The girl who invited me to the church had invited me to a meeting with a group of young women. The group was for women to commit themselves to God by being celibate. I enjoyed the meetings and wanted to join, but I was with my boyfriend. God gave me a way out of the situation, but I turned it down to please a man. I prayed and wanted help and when help came, I was scared. I cried at the last meeting I went to with the girls because of conviction. I knew God was calling me to something higher. The Bible says God does not tempt people to sin; temptation comes from within us and our own desires, not God. I desired to have a boyfriend and not be alone, but that desire just led to more heartbreak.

The Lord Is My Shepherd

Trapped! After one bad relationship, I thought I was free, but indeed I was still trapped. While in college, I met a man at a club and over time he became my boyfriend. He was a drug dealer. One night, I went over to his parent's house and we got into an argument. He was so upset he would not let me leave the house. The commotion was so loud that eventually his parents came into the room. After a while of them trying to convince him to let me leave the house they called his aunt and uncle over. Every time I tried to leave, he tried to grab me and even attempted to choke me several times. His parents had to grab him off of me multiple times. I tried calling the police and running out of the house, but nothing worked. During the midnight hour, I asked his mom to bring me a Bible. I opened it and could not remember the chapter in Psalms that my mother always read, Psalms 23. Raised in the Church, baptized in the Church and when I needed the

Word my mind failed me. In the chaos, I was trying to find peace and comfort. All that was in the room that night was confusion and anger. That morning, around 6:00 a.m., after being trapped, fighting, running, and crying, his parents called the cops on him and I was free.

Fight the Good Fight of Faith

Arrested! Bad relationships, bad friendships, bad roommates and bad choices. Choices, everyone has them. God gave us the right to have a choice, even when our choices go against Him. Sophomore year, I didn't get the roommate of my choosing, but we tried to make it work. A series of small offenses led to an altercation. Every Friday, I usually worked at Food Lion, but this one Friday I was off the schedule. I was going to cook, but when I looked for my spices, they were gone. She had taken my spices and placed them in her cabinet. When I confronted her, she lied and said they were hers. Voices raised and fingers waving! Then I was mushed in the face and we began to fight. When the fight was over, she ran out with bruises on her head and my finger was bleeding due to her biting it. I left the apartment, but my other roommate called me and said she had called the police. So I came back and the police officer arrested both of us.

I arrived at the station and I didn't cry until the magistrate said I could be kicked out of school. After being processed in, I was in the holding cell with all the other criminals unlike my roommate who had her own cell. I sat there thinking over and over, *How did I get here?* I was supposed to be at work, or cooking, or studying, but not arrested. I called my parents and we were eventually released because we were college students.

That weekend didn't get any easier for me! I stayed the night at my first boyfriend's house. The next morning, my finger was infected from her biting me. So, I took boyfriend's car to the hospital where the doctors told me I had to spend the night to let my thumb drain. When I told my boyfriend I had to stay overnight, he cursed me out because he needed his car. I remember crying alone in the hospital room, feeling like my life was crumbling.

I was in the hospital on Easter Sunday; while Jesus had risen, I was drowning in this season. I had to move out of my apartment and because I was the last to contact housing I got stuck in the worst dorm room. I remember crying over and over every night.

A couple of months went by and it was time to stand before the judge to know if I would have a record. I remember at my arraignment the judge was sentencing everyone. On the day of my case, my parents came to support me. There was a different judge and he dismissed the charges! I remember people clapping in the court room after he dismissed the charges. I wasn't fighting the good fight, but God was fighting for me!

During the beginning of the case, I heard there was another assault charge against me that I didn't know anything about. My roommate had called the cops on me before because I had pushed her. The reasons why do not justify my actions; I was wrong. So, I found myself back in the police station, turning myself in. I felt like I could not catch a break! This was not the freedom I expected when I left for college. However, after all these fights with my roommates and my boyfriends, I turned into a peacemaker. The day of my trial, my roommate never showed up. The judge ruled nolle prosequi! God gave me deliverance from all my troubles and when I was about 24, I got both charges erased from my record.

Transition: God Is Love

Conviction. Growing in God is never comfortable and after college I knew it was only God who pulled me through that season. However, I still wasn't sold out for Him. I was a lukewarm Christian, with one foot in the Church and the other in the world. I was still clubbing, drinking, and fornicating.

I remember the loneliness and embarrassment I felt walking into planned parenthood. I thought I was pregnant, so I made an appointment to take a pregnancy test. When I informed the person of the situation, they did not want to come with me. I remember sitting in the parking lot so stressed! This was a person who had I thought loved me, but it was nothing but lust! He didn't answer my calls all day until I texted him that I was not pregnant. After all these bad relationships, I still did not know my worth.

However, through the years I had encounters with the Lord and my love for God grew. I would carry my Bible around at work and study at home. I was healed and made whole in His love. Eventually, I met my husband; however, I was still fornicating. I remember one Sunday the presence was strong and I went into worship. When I came out of worship, I knew I had to stop fornicating. God convicted me because He wanted all of me and I was the apple of His eye. I told my fiancée what God wanted me to do and he took that walk with me. We decided to be celibate until marriage. I knew my worth this time and I wasn't going back.

Blessed Are Those Who Mourn

Testing! During this time in my life, I had finally developed a relationship with God where He was speaking to me; I was having dreams of angels and I knew the calling on my life. Life was good and then the Lord had to test my faith. When I heard my nephew had passed from heart failure, I lost my faith a little. My brother's only son. I remember the phone call from my mother crying on the other end and telling me I needed to go tell Roshaun. When I told my brother, he didn't believe me until my mother told him over the phone. As we stood in his kitchen I said, "Let's pray," and he decided to pray, which he rarely did. Until my parents lost him no one really understood his pain. The pain of losing a child.

Leading up to the week my nephew died, we had just buried my husband's mother on a Saturday. Three days later, death was knocking back on the door. I was emotionally and spiritually drained. Some days I was just going through the motions. I did not want to pray; I didn't want to read scripture. I just felt numb. I was smiling on the outside but mourning on the inside. How could the Lord let such a good kid die? I questioned God, knowing there would be no answer.

At his funeral, I remember I screamed. I was trying to hold in the pain so no one could see it, but the pain escaped anyhow. My heart felt broken, but God mended it with my first baby girl. Over the years, I never really brought up my nephew to my brother. I always wished him Happy Father's Day, but otherwise I was too scared to bring such a sensitive topic up.

For When I Am Weak, Then I Am Strong

Healed. My brother was around 19 when he was diagnosed with schizophrenia. At the time I was nine years old. I remember him not coming home for days and my parents not knowing where he was. Mental illness did not run in our family, so the diagnosis was surprising. My parents and I always thought it was drug related because in later years he came out of that diagnosis through much prayer but was never his old self.

My brother before his diagnosis was a great big brother. He worked hard at his construction job and always bought me things. We would drive around looking at the big houses and I learned all the shortcuts in Virginia Beach because of him. He would take me fishing sometimes at Stumpy Lake. Roshaun was a humble and cool guy.

Years later, he struggled a lot. When his only son passed away, things didn't get any easier. On July 23, 2022 he was taken from this earth by a heart attack. I remember the call from my mother and I asked her, "Where is he?" I felt like the protector and the big sister after his illness. The day of his death I remember hearing a still small voice say, "Roshaun." I meant to call him, but I got busy with life. Then to get the news that night I always wondered if it would have been different if I would have called him.

Losing a loved one makes you question a lot of things. People said how strong I was, but I had two parents who had just lost their son, so I felt someone had to stand strong. In reality, this was the hardest thing I have ever had to process. I remember going to the doctor because I was fatigued; I'd had my first anxiety attack, my vision was blurry where I was seeing stars, I had headaches and other things, but in reality I was depressed. I had never dealt with depression, so I didn't know the symptoms. In this part of my life, I knew nothing, but God could pull me out of this slump. God sent me dreams of my brother smiling and fishing. He reassured me my brother was okay! God was my rock and my fortress. When I was weak, He was my strength. When the valley was dark, He was my light! His Word was a lamp to my feet and a light to my path.

Conclusion:

I wanted to give up so many times, but my mom instilled in me not to be a quitter. Sometimes it feels easier to stay in your insecurity, depression, or terrible relationship, but God's plans are to prosper and not harm you. I thank God for every test and trial because it made me mature and complete! I almost gave up, but who would have thought I'm still standing, smiling, and glorifying God!

Jaleesa's Acknowledgements:

This book would not have been possible without Dr. Natasha's vision, so I would like to thank her for entrusting me with this assignment. Also, I owe an immense debt of gratitude to my parents who support me in all my endeavors. Lastly, to my husband, who loves me unconditionally. Thank you!

Jaleesa Olds

Jaleesa Olds is a Health Physicist for the federal government. She has a BS in Chemistry from VCU and a Masters in Business Administration from the University of Phoenix. She is a devoted wife and a loving mother to three beautiful daughters.

Her passion for the homeless led her to start a nonprofit called Fruitful Blessings Inc. Established by Jaleesa and her mother, Fruitful Blessings serves the homeless by providing meals and has mini pantries in three schools providing snacks bags and supplies. Jaleesa enjoys crabbing, fishing and gardening when she is not busy with work. She attributes her success to God being her solid foundation.

Contact Information

Instagram:

Jt_favor or frutifulblessings5

Facebook: Jaleesa Olds

Website: www.frutifulblessings5.org

Strengthened in the Struggle

Nicole Shrieves

"Life can be challenging at times. There are things beyond our control, but we have a God that is faithful and will comfort us in our times of need. Be encouraged, and don't give up. Even though we don't understand WHY, we know that all things work together for the good of those who love the Lord and who are called according to his purpose." ***(Romans 8:28)***

"Serenity Prayer"

March 18, 2011. A close friend died from injuries suffered in a motorcycle accident.

August 7, 2011. My best friend's first grandchild died at birth.

August 15, 2011. My son and nephew were arrested and charged with a Class 1 Felony.

September 11, 2011. My mother died from complications of renal and congestive heart failure.

I almost gave up – BUT GOD

"God, grant me the serenity to accept the things I cannot change":

Death is a perfect example of one of those things that we cannot change.

Death says, "It's final; it's done; it's over!"

Death does not discriminate. Race, sex, religion, or social and economic status will not give anyone an advantage because it will surely happen to each of us at some point in time.

Losing someone you love causes you to pause and reflect on your own life—and fear, dread, and sorrow will either consume you or force you to grow stronger.

Death is an action, but grief is an emotion and each person processes their emotions differently. In 2011, my friend died tragically, my God-grandchild died unexpectedly, and my mother died of natural causes. I processed each incident differently. My first reaction was to ask God WHY? Why do some people die in the prime of their lives? Why do babies die? I know that we aren't meant to live forever, but I still wanted to know WHY.

My best friend and I were expecting our first grandchildren in 2011. My granddaughter was born June 20, 2011 and my friend's grandbaby was expected to be born in August. We were both excited about becoming first-time grandmothers and had a lot of plans for doing grandparent things together. I remember receiving the phone call from her saying that the baby didn't make it. I was in shock and total disbelief. I prayed and asked God to give her strength as she consoled her daughter and processed her own emotions.

God's plan was different from our plans and, although we didn't understand it, we knew that everything happens for a reason. By this time, my granddaughter was about two months old and, although I was so proud of having my first grandbaby, I was also saddened because my best friend was grieving the loss of hers.

My grandbaby became the anchor in the raging storm that was just about to begin. God knew I would need something/someone to hold me down. Little did I know that in the next few weeks I was going to face the toughest battles yet and my time would be spent between visiting the jail and the grave. My son and nephew were arrested within a week of my friend losing her grandbaby. My mother died less than a month after their arrest.

My mother passed away at the age of 79 years old. She suffered from congestive heart failure and kidney disease. I remember being at her bedside a few days before she passed. She said, "Nicky, I'm tired."

I said, "Ma, go ahead and get some rest."

She looked at me and said, "No, baby, I'm tired." At that moment, I realized that my mom was the "tired" that needed peace and that was her way of telling me that she was ready to let go.

I had always heard how hard it was too lose a parent so I anticipated this great sadness, but my mother's death was different. I saw her suffer with pain and I was by her side through numerous hospitalizations and treatments. I understood that quality of life was more important than quantity of life. I asked God why I didn't have this overwhelming feeling of sadness and he spoke. "There was no unfinished business."

Think about that! No unfinished business. Although death says, "It's final; it's done; it's over," it makes grief a little more bearable when there's no unfinished business.

I had already dealt with so many losses that year that I was numb. I was tired and I desperately needed rest and peace, but, as they say, God doesn't put more on you than you can bear, right?

It took serenity to accept the things I could not change, BUT despite everything that I had faced, I chose to grieve, I chose to rest and I chose to live.

"The courage to change the things I can":

Grieving over someone who still has breath in their body is a different type of grief, but it can be just as heartbreaking.

If you've ever had a child or family member who has been or is currently incarcerated, you've probably experienced this type of grief. Unlike losing someone due to death, people tend to sympathize less with you and say things like, "Well, at least you can still go visit them," or, "At least you can talk to them on the phone." Although I do believe that their intentions are sincere it doesn't do much for someone who knows what those 10–30 minute visits and five-minute phone calls are really like.

I've sat on both sides of the courtroom, hoping for justice for a victim of a crime and praying for mercy when my loved ones were the perpetrators of a crime. If the wages of sin is death, I am so thankful that it was jail cell instead of the grave for my son and nephew. Jail saved their lives! And I am a firm believer of that!

I used to hear my mama say that when your children are young, they are on your feet but when they get older, they are on your heart. I never really understood what this meant until I became a mother of teenage/adult children and spent numerous sleepiness nights wondering where my children were and what they were doing when they were not in my sight.

I was active in church during the time of my son's and nephew's arrests. I remember going to church the week after it came out in the local news and no one asked if I was okay or offered to pray for my family. I could understand if they were shocked by the news and even disappointed by what our boys were accused of, but this was a place that preached God's grace and mercy and that we are all sinners and fall short of God's glory, so on and so on, BUT they failed miserably at practicing what they preached when I needed it most.

BUT God… My personal relationship with God became stronger! My prayers and communication with Him became more intimate than ever. I rededicated myself to Him whilst riding down Lankford Highway. The song "God's Will" by Darius Brooks came on the radio and the words ministered to my soul. The song ministered to me! One verse said, "I will cry until you tell me, let it go and let it, Because I know your will is what's best for me." At that moment, I knew and believed that all I had gone through and lost and all that I was to face was His will and He would carry me through it all.

I started my days off by reading Philippians 4:6. I spent less time entertaining other folk's opinions about what I should and shouldn't do when it came to my child. My relationship with God was first and foremost and no man/woman had power over heaven or hell so I was determined that if I or we as a family were going to get through this then I had to surrender it all to Him.

As I did just that! The road wasn't easy and, trust me, the devil was busy throughout the whole time, but I never lost faith that whatever the outcome would be, God had already written the story.

Never give up on your children! Love them despite their faults and imperfections because God has never given up on us. Don't only pray for the person affected by a crime, but pray for the perpetrator and all families that are involved. Send an encouraging word to someone who is incarcerated; you will be surprised how God can use incarceration as a way of drawing them closer to Him.

This was not the plan that I had hoped for my son and my nephew, but once again, God's plans are not always our plans.

It took courage to change the things I could … I chose to forgive, I chose to love and I chose to live.

"And the wisdom to know the difference":

Never underestimate the importance of self-care and self-perseverance.

Before you take off on a plane, the pilot announces that in the event of an emergency you should put your own mask on first before you try to put one on others.

HALT- Hungry, Angry, Lonely, and Tired

I saw this acronym a few years ago and it really spoke to me. It said if you are feeling one of them, take care of it right way, but if you are feeling two or more, HALT. According to the Oxford Dictionary, halt means to stop; cease moving, operating, etc., either permanently or temporarily.

The more I thought about it the more I began to relate. I've been hungry and by eating that need was met. I've been angry and by calming down that need was met. I've been lonely and by calling a friend that need was met. I've been tired and by getting a good night's sleep that need was met, but have you ever been tired and angry at the same time or lonely and angry? Or even hungry, tired, and angry all at the same time? Which need do you take care of first? This is when it becomes necessary, not optional but necessary, for you to HALT.

The body has a way of telling us that enough is enough. That's when sickness and depression will try to sneak in. Practice self-care and seek help, either from clergy, a professional therapist, or a trusted friend or family member. Never be ashamed to admit that you are "tired."

Just know that, as Isaiah 43:1 states, God knows us by name and we are His. He promised to see us through our struggles, whether it's the despair of grief or fear of tomorrow. God will never leave or forsake us no matter how many times we may want to give up.

You have a choice; you can choose to love, you can choose to forgive, you can choose to grieve and you can choose to live.

That's the wisdom to know the difference.

May the words of the Serenity Prayer bring you peace.

God, grant me the serenity

to accept the things I cannot change,

the courage to change the things I can

and the wisdom to know the difference.

Nicole's Acknowledgements

To my children—Taquan, Devonte, and Terique. My prayer is that you will put God first and lean on Him for guidance and protection. I pray that you live life to the fullest and realize that no matter how many times you fall down, you have a choice to get back up! I love you guys more than you will ever know!

To my grandbabies—Asiyah, Milan, Tristin and, Tayla. You are my pride and joy, my favorite people in the whole wide world, and Cole-Cole loves you more than you will ever know.

To my brothers and sisters—Tom, Van, Bessie, Wayne, Shirlene, and Carmela.

I can't tell you how blessed I am to have loving and supportive siblings. You guys are truly a blessing and I know I can always depend on you and for that I say I love you.

To Stacey. I'm so proud to call you my best friend. From the day I met you in kindergarten, you've always been by my side. We've grown up but not apart and through all of life's challenges it's a blessing to have a TRUE friend and for that I say I love you!

To Bishop David Sabatino. Thank you for hosting the Aspiring Authors workshop in 2023. I had the opportunity to meet many wonderful local authors and learn a lot about the process of writing a book. To my amazement, I learned that being a part of an anthology was a great way to start as an aspiring author.

Last but not least, to my classmate, my sister in Christ Dr. Natasha Bibbins.

Thank you for allowing me to be part of this anthology. Thank you for thinking of me and praying for me! Thank you for your vision to write this book and inspire others never to give up despite the obstacles they may face. May the testimonies shared in this book be a blessing to countless people so they too can say, "I didn't give up and life has become more fulfilling ever since." For that I say thank you!

Nicole Shrieves

Nicole Shrieves was born in Bayside, a small community within the town of Onancock located on the Eastern Shore of Virginia.

She is the youngest of six children born to William and Lois Marie Riley-Shrieves.

She is the mother of three sons, Taquan, Devonte, and Terique,

and a proud grandmother of four—Asiyah, Milan, Tristin, and Tayla.

For the past 32 years, Nicole has worked in various roles serving individuals with intellectual and developmental disabilities. She is currently a Developmental Services Support Coordinator.

Nicole's hobbies are spending time with her grandchildren, traveling, and thrift shopping.

A quote to live by. "I give because I have—I have because I give" (the late Jessie Poulson, Lifetime educator; Metropolitan United Methodist Choir Director).

Nicole is the owner of A Promise Kept, LLC, an agency that provides private duty nursing care to elderly and disabled individuals in the comfort of their home.

Favorite Scriptures:

Philippians 4:6 *Be anxious about nothing, but in every situation, by prayer and petition, with thanksgiving, present your requests to God and the peace of God that transcends all understanding will guard your hearts and minds in Christ.*

Psalms 46:10 *Be Still and know that I am God.*

CONTACT INFORMATION

Facebook: Nicole.L.Shrieves

Email: Nicole.Shrieves@yahoo.com

BECOMING
Carla D Manuel

Introduction

I had always dreamed of becoming a wife and mother, living in a house with a white picket fence. That was the only thing I aspired to be. Though it may be a shallow statement, it was true. Now, even though I dreamed of this, I surely didn't live my life in such a way that it would bring that dream to fruition. The reputation I had gained was far from what any man would want from a wife or a mother.

Even though I was living my life recklessly, deep in my heart I still believed it could happen. Eventually, I would meet a man who I thought would make that dream come true. But it was not without some hurt and pain along the way. You see, the enemy can make everything look good. It will look as if it's a great and amazing thing.

The enemy will help you do your sinning without any guilt, shame or self-doubt. That's why you have to be careful. We must remember that evil will disguise itself as good. Let me tell you; this relationship was gut-wrenching, but it was necessary for the woman I would become. I had to transform. The Apostle Paul urges us to be "transformed by the renewing of our minds" (Romans 12:2). I would have to change my thinking. I would have to become new. When we are becoming, we are in motion and moving along a path. We are realizing our potential as God's creation. We're on the way to flourishing as never before. I chose to go down this path, thinking I could win in a situation that was not right from the beginning. I have to be real and tell y'all that I had in my little warped mind, that this was my fairy tale. Well, it was not.

So, journey with me as I take you on a trip down memory lane. I will show you how I almost gave up on my dream of becoming a wife, a good mother, and a homeowner. Just keep in mind that what I went through was my plan, not God's plan. But God!

Jeremiah 29:11 KJV

For I know the thoughts that I think toward you, saith the Lord, thoughts of peace, and not of evil, to give you an expected end.

Chance Encounter

This day would start like any other. Up cleaning my house, singing, and then taking the children to the playground. While out there with the children, I decided to stop in on my bestie for a visit. When I entered her apartment, she had the company of her male cousin who was visiting from out of town. She introduced me to him; we talked for a while and then I left. The next day, she let me know that her cousin was interested in getting to know me and she asked if she could give him my number. Of course, I said yes.

The next day, we talked for hours. We would spend most of our days talking and getting to know each other. We talked about God and how He always kept us, even in our mess. Now, I have always been an open book, so I told him all about myself so there would be no surprises for him. He then, in return, told me all about himself and the state of his life too. He let me know that he was separated but not yet divorced. Now, that was a waving red flag, but I ignored it and just kept on talking.

There were many obstacles for both of us, but we decided to proceed with this courtship. Now, this was normal behavior for me. It really didn't matter about the obstacles. I would always jump the hurdles of life.

Soon after talking for days, we made a plan to meet. He would be traveling to see me. You see, even though there were some red flags on both of our parts, we still chose to ignore them. But more importantly, we chose to ignore God. Yes, we both knew better, but we chose to carry on. It was doomed from the beginning because we were totally out of line.

Jeremiah 17:5 KJV

Thus, saith the Lord; Cursed be the man that trusteth in man, and maketh flesh his arm, and whose heart departeth from the Lord.

Pretty Woman

The day came when he visited me. I had made arrangements with my mother to babysit my children for the weekend, and I got up and got dressed. The knock came at the door, and there he was, standing there tall and debonair, and his cologne was mesmerizing. We embraced and I welcomed him into my apartment. We had previously discussed going to the mall and then to a nightclub. I had said during that conversation that I didn't have anything to wear. So, we went to a store, and he purchased me a navy-blue and white Nike tennis set, and white Nike sneakers and we went about our day riding and singing. We went to the club and danced all night. It was amazing. I was not used to this type of man; just taking me out, wining and dining me while expecting nothing in return. I was shocked. I was prepared to let him stay the night, which was my usual, but he was a gentleman, and he chose to decline. He told me he would be staying at his cousin's house. That move really had me intrigued.

The next morning, he called and told me to get dressed; he said he was taking me somewhere. So, I got dressed, and when I got to the car, he had my bestie, who was his cousin, with him. We drove to the store. When we got inside, he told me to shop. I was dumbfounded. I said, "Huh?"

He repeated, "Shop, you need clothes, right?"

I replied, "Yes," then asked, "What can I get and how much can I spend?"

He looked at me and said, "Let me help you."

I stood there in shock and he began shopping for me. I was flabbergasted. I proceeded to try on outfit after outfit, coming out of the dressing room modeling while he and my bestie gave the yay or nay to the clothes and shoes. I was in shock, y'all. A whole new wardrobe! I felt like I was Julia Roberts in the movie Pretty Woman and he was Richard Gere. I wasn't on Rodeo Drive, but it sure felt like it. My heart was full. No one had ever treated me this good. I had only known him for a few weeks and he was treating me better than all the men I had dated for years.

My heart was full. Was this it? Had God been listening to me? Was He blessing me with the man of my dreams? I was truly smitten. He had won my heart. Later that day, he had to leave but promised to return in a couple of weeks. Y'all bless my heart. I was so caught up that I actually thought God was in that. A married man, though separated, is still a married man. Nope, that's not from God. But surely I thought it could be. Poor silly little me.

1 Peter 5:8

Be sober, be vigilant; because your adversary the devil, as a roaring lion, walketh about, seeking whom he may devour.

Whirlwind Romance / Tragedy

Soon after, we were having a full-blown love affair. He traveled often to see me and I traveled to see him. Things were great! We had the best time.

We always played "Street Thing" by Aayliah and sang to each other. We always dressed alike and we were all over the place together. His family loved me; we could not be divided. It was always us against them. He could always be heard yelling, "Who you with?"

I would always be laughing and saying, "You."

We both were having the time of our lives. This went on for a while, but eventually the distance was too much. We had a few hiccups and would split up a time or two, but we would always wind up back together again. The connection was strong. We always found our way back to each other. So many women wanted him because they saw how great he treated me. They pursued him.

Eventually, he chose to deal with someone we both knew. They would have an entanglement and we would split for good. We completely stopped speaking and then a unimaginable tragedy struck. His wife passed away. My bestie called and notified me that he had lost his wife and had to go retrieve his younger children. I reached out to him, offered my condolences, and told him I might come to the service with my bestie. He said, "OK," but I eventually chose not to go. I would later learn that he was in a relationship with someone he had known earlier in life. Even though we had not seen each other for a while, I always thought we would end up back together.

But we did not. I would be lying if I said this didn't bother me. I truly thought it would be me whom he chose. Later, someone who knew us both would inform me that he said he loved me but he couldn't be with me because he couldn't follow his heart. Instead, he needed to use his mind and marry someone he felt would be a great mother to his children. (I'm not sure if that statement was true. It was secondhand info) I must admit that I didn't understand that at the time. But how could I understand? I had not sought God, nor did I love myself or know what real love was. What was I feeling? I don't know, but I really did believe it was love. I felt the pain of betrayal. I was so lost that I almost gave up on ever loving or becoming that which I dreamed.

Psalm 34:18

The LORD is close to the brokenhearted and saves those who are crushed in spirit.

Becoming

After this happened to me, I never thought I would have my dream. But what I now realize is that God was preparing me and giving me a chance to become. Become means to evolve, change into, or emerge as something. As I look back at that situation, I see that God caused all things to work together for my good even though it did not feel good. Even though I made the choice to sin God still showed me grace and mercy.

I have always done self-examination and when reflecting on that situation, I realized that the man I wanted used his mind and at that time, he felt I was not adequate enough to raise his children, which was the most important thing to him. I can truly say that, at that time, he made the right choice.

That chapter in my life truly prepared me to become a better mother and wife.

I can look back at those days and see the watering from that time. That situation was growing on me. I can sit today in retrospect and say that God knew the plan He had for me and He would bring the right person into my life to help me become in all areas. I needed the right person to plant in my life so God would allow me to meet my husband.

Back then, I had children, but I was not a good mother. I could have been wife material, but I treated myself as less than that. I could have had a home, but I did not set my life up that way. But the man who chose me took time to teach me and help me become. What I also learned from this situation was to keep praying and never give up. I almost gave up on my dreams, y'all, but who would have thought that a major heartbreak would lead me to become the woman of God I am today, to be the good mother I am today and to own my home? God increased me.

One watered, one planted, but GOD gave the increase.

1 Corinthians 3:6–7 KJV

I have planted; Apollos watered; but God gave the increase. So then neither is he that planteth any thing, neither he that watereth; but God that giveth the increase.

Wait, I Say, on the Lord

I share with you these words of wisdom.

In this life we will willingly sin, make mistakes and unknowingly sin.

The most important thing you will ever do is give your life to Christ.

Will you be perfect? No.

But we must repent daily and strive to abide with Christ Jesus.

Listen, God knows all about your dreams and aspirations and if it is His will for your life, He will bring it to pass. Now, God's timing is not our timing. So we have to stay in constant communication so that we can hear from God and not be called away from our own lust. The Bible tells us in **James 1:14** *"But every man is tempted, when he is drawn away of his own lust, and enticed."*

We cannot go ahead of God. We may feel that we need to help Him, But God doesn't need our help and He certainly doesn't need us to go ahead of Him in disobedience.

Waiting and trusting in God can be hard, but running ahead of Him is worse.

When you go ahead of Him, you not only lose your peace, but you also waste time and then you have to face the repercussions of not trusting in God's timing. Moving ahead of God is DISASTROUS; as you can see above, it led to much heartbreak for me.

Also, sometimes things won't come to pass because it is not God's will for your life. You see, we want what we want but God knows what we need. He knows that our greatest need isn't to get what we want out of life but to get more God into our life.

We really need God more than we think and if we're totally honest with ourselves, one of the best ways for us to see our need for Him is when we look back over our life and see all of our heartbreaks and unfulfilled dreams.

God ALWAYS knows what's best for us. He tells us in **Isaiah 55:8–9 KJV** "For my thoughts are not your thoughts, neither are your ways my ways, saith the Lord.For as the heavens are higher than the earth, so are my ways higher than your ways,and my thoughts than your thoughts."

So always seek God and wait to hear from Him. We have to wait on God and be sure it is the plan He has for our life.

Psalm 27:14 "Wait on the Lord: be of good courage and he shall strengthen thine heart: wait, I say, on the Lord."

Note to Oneself

Looking back over my life, there was a common denominator … a man.

The man, the man, the man. There was a pattern. I always felt that I was doing what I wanted to do, but I have come to realize there was some type of deficit within. As you grow in age, life, wisdom, and your relationship with God, you will learn that there is no limit to what you can do. Learn to love God and then love yourself. Know who you are. You have to value yourself.

Remember, you teach others how to treat you. The saying "You are what you attract" is a concept that suggests that people attract what they believe they deserve and that their beliefs have a significant impact on their lives. It can also mean that people attract things that are a reflection of what is inside them. So always work on you. Become the best version of you. Let your dreams and aspirations be bigger than your capabilities and any fears you may have. You have to see it before you can see it. Write it down so you can go back and look at it.

Habakkuk 2:2

"And the Lord answered me, and said, Write the vision, and make it plain upon tables, that he may run that readeth it."

If you see it written, it will stay in the forefront of your mind. It causes you to take notice. Also, watch what you say. We must remember that there is life and death in the power of the tongue. Speak life. Always speak the Word of God as you prepare, study, and pray. God hears His Word and is always willing to perform it.

Don't give up. I almost gave up because I wasn't in the right standing with God, nor was I seeking Him. I knew of God, but I didn't have a relationship with Him.

When you go about life doing whatever you want to do without God, it can really cause you some great pain and suffering. I put myself through a lot. I almost gave up, but who would have thought God would extend His grace, have mercy on me, and bless me still? Yes, he loves us so much that He will give us the desires of our heart despite what you have done or will do. God is amazing.

1 Corinthians 13:4–8. NIV

Love is patient, love is kind. It does not envy, it does not boast, it is not proud. It does not dishonor others, it is not self-seeking, it is not easily angered, it keeps no record of wrongs. Love does not delight in evil but rejoices with the truth. It always protects, always trusts, always hopes, always perseveres. Love never fails.

Conclusion

Do you want to accept Christ today? If so, say these words out loud and believe them in your heart.

"Dear God, I know I am a sinner. I want to turn from my sins and I ask for Your forgiveness. I believe that Jesus Christ is Your Son. I believe He died for my sins and that You raised Him to life. I want Him to come into my heart and to take control of my life. I want to trust Jesus as my Savior and follow Him as my Lord from this day forward. In Jesus' Name, amen."

If you said these words out of your mouth and believe them in your heart you are saved. This is the first step. Now you have to cultivate this relationship with Him. Make Him first in everything. Yes, it is a process and we all will be working toward perfection until the day He comes back. But keep striving. Daily we must repent and seek Him.

All my life, I have been transparent (God made me that way), so being that way with God is easy for me. Actually, it should be easy for us all because God knows everything anyway. Remember, there is nothing to hide. Transparency is where the blessings reside.

I find that people have a hard time with this in the world for fear of judgment. Not from God but from man. But fear not, for God is with you. By the way, the people are gonna judge you anyway. In case you didn't know, half of the stuff you hide and are ashamed of, the people already know you did it and some have done it too and think that they hid from people, but trust me, somebody knows.

Listen, there is freedom in transparency and I find that God can use you freely. So as you grow in God, don't be afraid to share your testimony as God leads. You never know who you may help.

John 8:32 KJV

"And you shall know the Truth and the Truth shall make you free."

As I close, I pray that this will help you in your walk with Christ. Ask God to forgive you and do not be ashamed.

The Bible tells us that only God can forgive us so ask Him for forgiveness. Listen, shame is a profound emotional experience, often arising from sin, disobedience, or failure to meet divine standards, characterized by feelings of guilt, embarrassment, or disgrace, and can be both a personal and communal experience. Shame doesn't come from God. It is a tool of the adversary. The enemy uses shame to keep us in despair, but God gives us hope by showing us the error of our ways and His Word evoking change and repentance. So don't wallow in it. That's why we should share our testimonies because we are overcome by the blood of the Lamb and our testimonies.

You should always try to be real and transparent. You can always be real and transparent with God.

Go to Him with all of your broken pieces. God is the potter and we are the clay and if we go before Him, lay our souls bare and give Him all our brokenness, He will put us back together again.

2 Samuel 22:21

"GOD made my life complete when I placed all the pieces before him." (MSG)

Change your thinking. Release the past stigma and labels that others put on you and that you've put on yourself.

Let the old man die and let God resuscitate you. Who you were before Christ is not who you are after Christ. Once you accept Christ, a change will take place. The old you is gone and you become a new creature. We've all messed up. But through it all, because of Christ, we have been redeemed. God has taken our sins and forgiven them not to be remembered again. So, ask yourself a question. If God forgave and forgot your sins, then why are you remembering them?

Hebrews 8:12

For I will be merciful to their unrighteousness, and their sins and their iniquities will I remember no more.

I am so glad that God extended grace and mercy to a sinner like me and loved me so much that He allowed me time to come to Him and become.

Because she established a relationship with God and changed.

She would BECOME!

I am SHE Who would have thought?

Carla's Acknowledgements

God—who knew me before I was formed in my mother's womb. Whose grace, mercy and unconditional love sustain me. The head of my life. The ONLY ONE who reigns supreme in my world. I want to thank you, God, for everything.

My Husband—Rickey Manuel

I love you. I'm everything I am because you loved me. I thank God you found me.

My Children

To my children and my grandchildren. Forgive me for the mistakes I have made. I am sorry for the unhealed parts of me that may have hurt you. It was never a lack of love for you, only a lack of love for myself. I pray that my growth and repentance to God has now allowed you to heal the parts of you that were broken.

You all are the best of me.

To My Son in Heaven:

TaNie Shaheed Kees, you are missed beyond measure. Continue to watch over your mommy.

To Two of My Besties

Sharon Ames Brown and Tasha Berg, what can I say? You have been a friend tried and true. You have never changed.

It doesn't matter how much time has passed, we always pick up where we left off. Strong friends in the world and even STRONGER friends for the Lord! So from the words of the song "Best Friend":

Friends may come, and friends may go, But you should know that That I've got your back, it's automatic. So never hesitate to call 'Cause I'm your sister and always for ya.

I Love you, my friends.

To my sister Dr. Natasha Bibbins, I love you. Thanks for this opportunity. **You and me us never part.**

To the Readers

Thank you and I pray this book will help you heal and lead you to Christ.

Always remember this quote from Tony Evans: "God will meet you where you are in order to take you where He wants you to go."

Carla D Manuel

Carla D Manuel is a God-fearing woman. She is the daughter of Vincent Smith and Rebecca Collins. She was born on the beautiful Eastern Shore of Virginia in a little city called Painter. She is married to Rickey Manuel. She is an Amazon Best-Selling Coauthor in the book *God Will Right Your Wrong Too*, which was compiled by Dr. Natasha Bibbins.

She is the mother of six children—Brandon, Rickia, Rodneyka (Muffin), Ta-Nie (RIP), Yahzmeen and Zion—and a nana to 14 grandchildren—Remi, Samir, Kasai, Khasheem, Kyzavion, Jake, Chosen (RIP), Zoey, Liam, Noah, Milani, Baby Manuel, Chance and Malik (aka Mufasa).

Carla holds BA in Theology and in August of 2020 received her license to officiate marriages.

She is a notary. She is the visionary for a group on Facebook for parents who have lost children called Hearts in Heaven.

Carla's favorite scripture is **2nd Corinthians 5:17**

Therefore, if any man be in Christ, he is a new creature: old things are passed away; behold, all things are become new.

She is living proof that God can change anybody!

Contact Information

Name: Carla Manuel

Email: cmanuel630@gmail.com

Facebook: Carla Manuel

Instagram: 2ThyOwnSelfBTrue

X: 2ThyOwnSlfBTrue

BUILT TO SURVIVE, CALLED TO THRIVE

Tanikwa S. Matthews

Mind over Matter

My life's end was staring at me in the mirror while the shower was running. Tears were flowing down my face as silent screams poured from my soul. The bathroom was my sanctuary to keep the boys from hearing me cry due to the pressures of life without causing them to worry. *These boys will be fine, they have one another,* my inner voice said. *Why, God, would you give me these four boys KNOWING I'm not equipped to take care of them?* My cries got louder and my tears flowed faster. *I need to just end this mess of a life I'm living.* My thoughts got louder in my mind and I started responding to them out loud. I got in the shower to cry and contemplate how I would end my life.

My oldest banging on the bathroom door took me out of my trance. Wiping my face and trying to change my voice I responded, "Yes, SonShine?"

He said, "Mommy, are you okay?"

I paused then tried to respond with a reassuring, "Yes SonShine, why do you ask?"

He said, "Mommy, you've been in the shower forever."

"I'm fine, SonShine. I'll be out in a few." I tried to reassure myself while responding.

A flood of thoughts raced through my mind. *Do I really want the boys to "find me" dead? Where would they go? Who would take care of them? Would they be angry with me? What would my family say? I know financially they will be set for life and have everything I couldn't give them.*

Immediately, tears turned into anger. Now, why did I want to end my life when God gifted me four blessings? And if I took my own life, they wouldn't be entitled to any life insurance so they wouldn't even be able to bury me. The mere fact was my life was in so much turmoil and I must still raise four boys alone. I was angry, sad, hurt, and wished life wasn't so challenging. I had no friends, family lived hours away, and going anywhere or doing anything with four boys cost entirely too much. *UGH, why, Lord, why do I have to struggle like this?* From the shower to the closet, I carried tears.

"Praise the Lord, my soul, and forget not all His benefits— who forgives all your sins and heals all your diseases, who redeems your life from the pit and crowns you with love and compassion…" (Psalms 103:2–4, NIV). These were the words I read when I opened the Bible.

Sadness turned to joy! Once again, I heard little hands knocking on the closet door. Then it slowly opened and all four of the boys came in. They sat next to me on the closet floor. Somehow, they could tell I had been crying. One by one they hugged me and reassured me they were there for me. I giggled. At that moment, I reflected on the joy God gave me through each of them. The next day, I woke up and read Joshua 1:9. "Have I not commanded you? Be strong and courageous. Do not be discouraged, for the Lord your God will be with you wherever you go." (NIV)

Months passed by. Early mornings and late nights took a toll on me and that 2:00 p.m. sleepiness crept in every day. I took frequent bathroom trips at work and found myself crying from sleep deprivation. As a full-time mother and servicemember I felt the systematic routine wearing down on me again. Sitting in the large bathroom stall, thoughts of "why me" started back in my mind. Yes, the bathroom was my "secret place". I had NO life. Waking up at 4:00 a.m., getting the boys dressed, packed, and dropped off in three locations. Then rushing through traffic to make the 6:15 a.m. PT formation. My only moment of reset was the seven-minute car ride to pick up the boys and head home to switch hats and be "Mom".

Lord, this can't be how you wanted my life to be. What happened to the big house with the wraparound porch and white picket fences from my childhood dreams? Waiting for the light to turn green into my boy's school I broke down crying once again, thinking I could just run into a ditch so I wouldn't have to feel the pain of not being equipped to be a mom of BOYS!

What can I possibly teach boys? They are so full of energy and every day they take the last drop of energy I have. Gathering the strength to turn into the parking lot and walk into the school was a big step for me. Then hearing the sweetest little voices screaming, "Mommy," interrupted my entire suicidal thought process. Clearly God had a reason for giving me all boys. Then I remembered a dream I had begging God for five boys...WHAT WAS I THINKING? Surely, God remembered my childhood request.

The Encounter

One day, while rereading my journal, I noticed I had written about how wonderful it was to go through the birthing process with each of the boys. God's voice whispered, "You are fully equipped go forth." Now, let me say I was a little scared at first, but in a peaceful way. Then I shouted because I recalled asking to hear the voice of God and He had spoken to me! Crying, shouting and so many thank you Gods filled my room. It was such a beautiful encounter. I imagined being at the feet of Jesus, worshipping and asking for forgiveness. I couldn't believe I had such selfish thoughts of ending my life because of hardship. I begged God to fill my heart with joy, compassion, and patience. Don't cringe because you read the word patience. I know what some of you may be thinking and you may be shaking your head and saying to be very specific when praying.

So, it felt like that patience I asked for began to come in many ways. From teaching the boys to tie their shoes 50 times a day to catching every red light while in a rush. Negative thoughts filled my mind. This time it was the belief that I wasn't worthy of God's patience. Although He had told me I was equipped, patience wasn't part of the deal, or so I thought. Talk about humbleness.

I went back to my journal again and I read my notes from a Bible study a few years prior. My focus went to the scriptures I had put arrows beside. My eyes rested on James 4:10: "Humble yourselves before the Lord, and he will lift you up in honor." (NIV) And my mind wondered, *Why are you telling me to humble myself, Lord? I get up, drop off my boys, go to work, come home, go to bed and start over the next day.* Let me tell you how I was scrambling to look up the word humble. According to Webster's, humble is characterized by recognizing one's dependence on God and not considering oneself greater than Him but rather as an obedient servant.

Of course I'm disagreeing with the definition concerning myself. Then, after rereading the definition a few more times, I realized that I had not been an obedient servant. Mainly because for a few years God had told me to speak, write, and, more importantly, read His Word daily. Yet I found every reason to believe that if I prayed, went to church and helped others I was good to go. NOT SO! God wanted more.

So I began reading the story of Job; realizing how much he lost yet he remained humble despite it all had me in tears. Crying and reading about the suffering he experienced, the misfortunes and multiple tragedies, I realized my life wasn't that bad after all. Job 3:1–4 reads, "Job opened his mouth and cursed the day of his birth. He said: May the day of my birth perish, and the night that said, a boy is conceived! That day—may it turn to darkness; may God above not care about it; may no light shine on it." (NIV) Whoa! My heart raced while I was reading this because I could relate. But Job suffered much more than I did. Come to think about it, I hadn't really suffered. We had the necessities and I was in my right mind. It was at that moment that I recognized how blessed I am for real.

There I was crying, complaining and wanting to end it all. I felt "stuck" with my boys to raise alone, people on who looked down on me, and broken self-esteem. Then I recalled how much Job SUFFERED a great loss and still humbled himself to God. I related so much to Job I would refer to myself as Jobette. Despite marital separation and raising four boys ages eight, four, two and 10 months at that time, God reminded me that my life has purpose. And regardless of how challenging life's journey can be, Father God makes provision and supplies all my needs.

Emotional Rollercoaster

I talked to my family about some of these challenges and my brother agreed to help me with the boys. Now, my military position had me traveling several times a month. On October 21st, 2010, I came home from taking my PT test. While getting the boys ready for school and childcare I began having severe chest pains. I remember falling flat on the floor and could hear everything but couldn't move. My oldest son called 911 and I heard the entire call but was vomiting and couldn't speak. I was taken to Laurel Regional Hospital. I remember Tyrell and Jordan coming to my bedside. I asked them to take care of their younger brothers and one another. Then Jeremiah and Antoine came in with my brother and I recall seeing the worry in their eyes as I leaned over to hug them.

The fluttering in my chest became more unbearable. Several doctors came running into my room and the machines started beeping louder and faster. I tried to speak but couldn't. The doctor kept asking for my name. In my mind I was screaming it, but nothing came out of my mouth. He then told me I was having a heart attack and I would need to be taken via medivac to Johns Hopkins. I heard the doctor call my parents telling them they needed to get to Johns Hopkins immediately.

My tears were the only words my heart could speak. *Is this the end? Did I fulfill my purpose here on Earth?* I wasn't ready to die yet. My boys were little and I hadn't accomplished the things on my dreams and goals list. I thought about all the bad things I did in life. Not one good thought came to my mind. It felt like I was having an out-of-body experience because I could see myself lying in the hospital bed in pain as I was sitting in the corner of the ceiling looking down.

I was back to thinking I should've just taken the bottle of pills so I wouldn't have to feel this pain. Just at that moment, one of my church friends came in and told the doctor she was riding with me in the helicopter and wouldn't take no for an answer. She prayed for me. My brother walked back in with a worried look, afraid to say anything, and he kept apologizing. I just shook my head to tell him it wasn't his fault. Thoughts continued racing through my mind one after another. I wanted to end it all. Then I remembered the story of Job.

The helicopter ride seemed like a long-distance flight, but I heard God's voice yet again. "Greater is he that is in me, than he that is in the world." (1 John 4:4) "God is IN ME," I shouted! Then I heard the song "He Has His Hands on You" playing on repeat in my mind. I couldn't believe I wanted to let go of my life again because of another roadblock. This emotional rollercoaster had to stop and when I got off, I would refuse to get back on. My friend started reading the scripture from 1 Corinthians 3:16–17: "Don't you know that you yourselves are God's temple and that God's Spirit dwells in your midst? If anyone destroys God's temple, God will destroy that person; for God's temple is sacred, and you together are that temple."

Upon arrival at Johns Hopkins, they ran several tests. I swear my parents, both four hours away, and my pastor beat the helicopter there. After days of tests and taking what seemed like all my blood, the doctor asked if I was stressed. I laughed while crying. He advised me to recognize that we all have stress-related factors and told me I needed to find ways to reduce stress. 2 Corinthians 4:17–18 reminds us, "for our light and momentary troubles are achieving for us an eternal glory that far outweighs them all. So we fix our eyes not on what is seen, but on what is unseen, since what is seen is temporary, but what is unseen is eternal." (NIV)

Moving in Purpose

While the doctor was talking, I saw my life flash before me. I thought about all the things that I'd done negatively, sins I committed, and the people I had hurt in life. I realized that my life is not my own and I was put here for a reason and purpose. I realized the importance of making sure that I was eating healthy and recognizing that we all have stress but it's how we handle it that matters most. Finding ways to manage stress in a positive manner was important to my overall health. When things got to a point where they seemed overwhelming, I read 1 Corinthians 10:13: "No temptation has overtaken you, except which is common to me, but God is so faithful he will never let you be tempted beyond what you can bear and even when you are tempted, he will provide a way out so you can endure it." (NIV).

Years went by and sometimes those suicidal thoughts tried to creep in when life's challenges came quickly towards me; I found solace in reading the scriptures that I wrote on index cards that I carried with me. Taking moments to breathe and going for a short walk to help relieve some of the stress. Philippians 4:13 leaped into my spirit: "I can do all things through Christ who strengthens me." (NIV) It's often stated that God will never put more on you than you can bear and I firmly believe that, although it's not written in scripture.

I recognize that God already laid the blueprint for my life while I was formed in my mother's womb. He knows every trial, tribulation, and challenge that we will face and He gives us the tools we need. So I must think that if God is in me everywhere I go, He walks with me and talks to me and gives me the strength to endure all hardships as a good soldier. It's **mind over matter** as you have **an encounter** with God on this **emotional rollercoaster** to keep **moving in purpose**. Even when any of life's challenges hit you hard God is right there. That is praiseworthy!

There are so many people suffering in silence who are embarrassed to express their feelings. Most times people tend to be closed off because someone close to them shared personal information without permission. Others believe people will view them as weak and tease them. Therefore, we need to be mindful about how we interact with one another and provoke one another to good works.

Using Navigation Properly

Most suicidal thoughts begin with depression. While many will deny they are depressed, there are warning signs. Some of these warning signs include:

1. Feeling hopeless and helpless
2. Having low self-esteem and/or mental health problems
3. Losing a loved one or ending a relationship
4. Increased feelings of guilt
5. Changes in mood or behavior
6. Giving away possessions

7. Emotional distress and anxiety

8. Bullying, such as race, gender, disability, and religious belief

9. Different types of abuse, including sexual, physical, emotional, mental, domestic and psychological

If you or a loved one are experiencing any of these indicators, connect with people you trust. It's fine to share your feelings if you're struggling. Don't allow the enemy to play tricks with your mind. Don't suffer in silence … PLEASE! Your life is worth it. Help is available 24 hours a day.

CALL OR TEXT 988 or visit the website 988lifeline.org

Let me share some additional ways to help overcome those thoughts:

1. Seek help!

2. Explore lifestyle changes like exercise and healthy eating

3. Maintain healthy social connections

4. Consider journaling and practicing relaxation techniques

5. Set realistic goals to regain a sense of control

Wake up with enthusiasm and positivity despite what may be happening around you. Take time to read the Bible, pray to God and speak positive affirmations over yourself. Look at yourself in the mirror, not at the imperfections and flaws but the beauty. Remind yourself of Psalm 139:14: "I praise you because I am fearfully and wonderfully made; your works are wonderful…" (NIV)

Here are some affirmations to say to yourself in the mirror:

1. I AM PURPOSEFUL
2. I AM WORTHY OF SUCCESS AND LOVE
3. I AM LOVED BY THE MOST HIGH GOD
4. I AM GIFTED
5. I AM CONFIDENT
6. I AM MOTIVATED AND A VESSEL FOR PEACE AND JOY
7. I AM CAPABLE AND STRONG
8. I AM CALM, AT PEACE AND CALM
9. I AM RESILENT AND EQUIPPED TO HANDLE WHATEVER COMES MY WAY
10. I AM DESTINED FOR GREATNESS

Say this prayer:

Lord, I thank you for another day filled with opportunities. Thank you for the breath of life, joy, health and strength. I am reminded of your goodness, mercy and grace. God, I thank you for your love and peace, which surpasses all my understanding. Your love encompasses me daily and I'm grateful for the gift of life. Enter into my heart, mind, and soul. Open doors that no man can shut and shut doors no man can open. I pray you equip me with the tools to fulfill the purpose you created in my life to do. God, you are gracious and your loving kindness is wonderful. Thank you for all the blessings you have afforded me. Thank you for your protection, provision and unconditional love. In Jesus' name, Amen.

Tanikwa's Acknowledgements

God, my Rock, my Sword and Shield, you planted me on this journey and I am grateful for every breath. Apostle Dr. Natasha Bibbins, you are a jewel and I would be remiss if I didn't say THANK YOU for your encouragement, motivation and continuous push for me to step out of my shell. To my family—Mom (Drucilla), Dad (Bennie), Grandmothers (Julia and Ella), Brothers (Dominic, Joshua and Brandon), Sister (Brittney) and Cousins (Andrew and Wanda)—each of you has a special place in my heart. To my "Fantastic Four"—Tyrell, Jordan, Jeremiah and Antoine—you are the best gifts I ever have received.

Tanikwa S. Matthews

Tanikwa S. Matthews, also known as "Coach T", is the oldest of six hailing from Philadelphia, PA. She is a God-fearing mother of four boys, a life coach, minister, and motivational speaker. She is the CEO and founder of two businesses—Women Achieving Victory Everywhere (WAVE), a 501(c)3 nonprofit organization for women, youth and military families, and HisNHersJewels, LLC, which creates an array of custom-designed handmade products.

Tanikwa is an author of five Amazon Bestsellers: Forces of Change: A Nonprofit Anthology, Words of Wisdom for the Heart and Soul volumes 1 through 4. She is an ambassador for Reign premium (plant-based) feminine products. She volunteers with the Northampton High School band and track team. Tanikwa is a team leader in the Relay for Life Annual Campaign honoring and remembering those diagnosed with cancer. She is a member of the Eastern Shore VA Chamber of Commerce. Tanikwa is a First Sergeant for

HHC 338th Medical Brigade with previous duties as an Executive Administrative Sergeant, Victim Advocate, Career Counselor, Unit Administrator, Postal Clerk and Protocol Liaison culminating in 28 years of U.S. Army active duty and reserve service.

Tanikwa hosts weekly Facebook and YouTube shows titled "Bridging the Gap from War 2 Wisdom" featuring guests experienced in a variety of backgrounds. Topics range from administrative support to mental health and youth initiatives. Tanikwa hosts monthly "Battle Buddy" workshops for youth ages 13–18 and wellness workshops for women. She has been featured in the Eastern Shore News, POWER magazine, WAVY TV 10, and Making Headline News. Tanikwa has been awarded "Positive Social Influence" by ACHI Magazine, Extraordinary Woman Award, Extraordinary Diva Award, Black Girl Magic Image Awards: Military Servant of the Year and nominated for Woman of Influence, Public Service, and Woman of Excellence.

Tanikwa enjoys spending time with family and friends and learning from her 94-year-old grandmother. Some of her other hobbies are reading, bowling, skating, dancing, networking, learning, crafting and cheering loudly at her son's sports/band events and for her Philadelphia Eagles! Her life lesson is derived from Galatians 6:9 and Joshua 1:9.

Feel free to follow my social media platforms:

Facebook:https://www.facebook.com/profile.php?id=100094081395463&mibextid=LQQJ4d

Instagram: https://www.Instagram.com/womenachievingvictorywave

YouTube: https://youtube.com/channel/UCVHAz1Xt4zBj8WwnAfiyGSw

Website: womenachievingvictory.org

TicTok: womenachievingvictory

Facebook: https://www.Facebook.com/HisandHersJewelsllc

Instagram: https://www.Instagram.com/Hisandhersjewelsllc

Reign: https://app.elify.com/vbc/vp0odvzohh?t=j6kzvk

TRUST THE PROCESS
Teka Giddens

God's Grace – Never Giving Up

What made me feel like giving up? Absolutely nothing! Not one single thing! No matter what I've endured, I have always known that God was with me. Even when life left me feeling burned, broken, and discarded, He never let me go. God sustained me, restored me, and reminded me that His grace was always greater than my grief (2 Corinthians 12:9).

When I sat down to write this chapter for the book, I tried to recall a time when I truly felt like giving up and I couldn't. Sounds strange, right? But that's the power of grace and mercy! It's almost comical that I could forget heartbreak, rejection, abuse, depression, and even thoughts of suicide. That's what happens when God steps in. He takes your pain and transforms it into purpose so powerfully that you don't even recognize the person you used to be and all that you've been through.

And just when I thought I was on a smooth road to sharing my testimony for this book, life started testing me all over again. Tested me personally, professionally, and spiritually.

Trials came from every direction, directly and indirectly, with people I love the most, forcing me to seek God like never before on a whole new level, not only for myself but for others too. It was as if God was saying, "Oh, you forgot what I brought you through? Let's see if your memory comes back when the next major test arrives!" We cannot become so numb to our past struggles that we forget WHO carried us through them. Life is STILL testing me as I type this passage right now. The enemy wants me to shut up and be afraid of my voice to distract me from my assignment and calling.

I now understand why I never truly considered giving up. God had His hand on my life from the very beginning "For such a time as this" (Esther 4:14). He knew that I would be called into ministry, not just through my personal testimony but through a Kingdom relationship (which, by the way, officially became a reality on March 9, 2025 in a surprise engagement at my now fiancé's Pastoral Installation Service that I had no clue about when I first started writing this passage for this book! Look at God! "Calling things that are not as though they were" Romans 4:17!).

God was saving His best for last and I had no idea. I knew that my parents raised me to be great, to be a pillar in the community, but I never realized that it was for God's Greatness until much later in life.

To anyone reading this who is still unsure of God's plan for your life, don't be discouraged. Your timeline is not a mistake. Some are called early while others, like me, don't fully grasp it until later. That doesn't make you less anointed, less chosen, or less worthy of The Call. Sometimes, our process takes longer because of our own detours. Other times, it's simply because God's perfect timing requires a season of preparation. But when you know, you know.

For those who have been called early, I know it's not easy. But count it as an honor! God saw something in you that needed to be activated sooner rather than later. You were chosen, recruited onto "His team", and given your "Kingdom uniform" before some even realized there was a team to join! No, it won't be easy, but you were chosen for a reason. You have the opportunity to fight the wiles of the enemy and bring more disciples to Christ. If I knew then what I know now … whew! Where would I be?

And to those still waiting, be encouraged; your time is coming. Stay faithful and stay the course. Your preparation, pressing and pruning season is not a punishment, it's a setup for something greater.

Childhood

From a young age, I was blessed to know about God. My mother made sure we were in church every chance we got. And while I didn't realize it then, she was laying the foundation for something that would sustain me for a lifetime. She worked tirelessly balancing her career and education while also being one of the best nurses around. She still made sure that our spiritual health was just as important as our physical well-being. My father, a dedicated law enforcement officer and then later an alternative education administrator, worked shifts that required tremendous sacrifice, discipline, and courage. He instilled qualities I later realized were also essential in my walk with Christ.

I sang in the Rosebuds Choir, participated in Christmas and Easter plays, and was baptized as a young child. I believed with all my little heart that Jesus died for me. Believing is one thing, but walking by faith is another.

At that age, I knew of God, but I didn't fully know Him. I had heard the stories of the Bible and the miracles of Jesus, but I had yet to experience my own testimony of faith. It wasn't until much later that I understood what it meant not only to acknowledge His presence but to actually make space for Him in my life. What it meant to surrender, to trust, to walk according to His will and to truly revere His power and might. There's a difference between knowing of God and truly knowing God. And the journey from one to the other is where the real transformation happens. I thank God for transformation.

As a child, my imagination ran wild. At night, I would lie in bed imagining what Heaven looked like. Streets of gold? Endless peace? No bedtime? (Now that was a place I wanted to be!) But in the same breath, I feared the unknown. The thought of death scared me. The idea that someone as great and mighty as God was able able to see my every move. He could see what I was doing even when my parents couldn't. That alone sometimes made me second-guess some of my decisions as a child. They said that Santa watched you in December, but God? He had 24/7 surveillance with no blind spots! You couldn't hide from Him, bargain with Him, or sneak cookies from Him like you could with your parents.

But even in my childlike fear and uncertainty, God knew. He knew what I would face. He knew the obstacles I would overcome. He knew the mistakes I would make and the lessons I would learn. He knew the path I would take, even the detours. And most importantly, He knew exactly who I would become.

Looking back, I thank God not just for the lessons but for the transformation. That moment when my faith moved beyond just knowing of Him and shifted into walking with Him. As I said before, there's a difference between growing up in the Church and growing in Christ. There's a difference between hearing about God and experiencing His presence. There's a difference between reciting scripture and truly living by it. When that shift happens, everything changes.

I had to live through some things before I could truly understand just how mighty His hand is and just how deep His love runs. But what I know now is this, God doesn't just want us to acknowledge Him. He wants us to walk with Him. He wants a relationship, not just a routine. He wants our faith, not just our fear. And when we finally say yes to Him, we unlock a life of peace, power, and purpose that is beyond anything we could have imagined as children.

So if you're still in that space of knowing of God but not quite sure you know Him, keep going. Keep seeking. Keep praying. Because when the moment of transformation comes, you'll look back and say, "Wow… Who would have thought?"

And the answer is—God did.

Teenage Years and the Journey Ahead

As I got older, life didn't slow down. If anything, it felt like someone hit the fast-forward button! My parents worked tirelessly to balance their careers while raising three highly energetic, overly involved, and slightly dramatic in their own way children that were born five years apart. There was my sister Keta (the oldest and the groundbreaker of what not to do and our idol growing up), me (the worker bee, the undisputed favorite, just kidding … maybe), and my baby brother GL (everyone's heart and the life of any party, of course). If there was an extracurricular activity, trust and believe we were in it!

Band? Check. Chorus? Absolutely. Basketball, T-ball, softball, baseball, track, volleyball, cheerleading? All of the above. And let's not forget park and recreation sports, AAU, Beta Club, Honor Society, homecoming court, student government. The list goes on and on!

But through all the chaos, one thing was certain; our parents never wavered in teaching us the importance of integrity, kindness, obedience, and respect for authority. (Although, let's be real, back then, it just felt like unnecessary rules standing in the way of our fun or just being mean!) What I didn't realize at the time was that they weren't just preparing me to be a well-rounded citizen, they were preparing me for my Kingdom Assignments. Every bit of discipline, structure, and, let's be honest—some well-deserved "laying on of hands" (Proverbs 13:24, spare the rod, spoil the child was definitely applied in our household) was part of a divine molding process.

At the time, I thought my parents were just keeping us in line, but looking back, I see now that they were equipping me for something far greater than just good manners and being a morally good person. They were instilling in me the values I'd need to walk into my purpose. Because as much structure as we had, no amount of extracurricular activities could prepare me for the real battles ahead. For that, I needed the Full Armor of God (Ephesians 6:10–18).

Coming up in school, one thing about me, I loved people. Not just liked, but loved. It didn't matter to me if you were Black, White, Hispanic, differently abled, the smartest in the class, the star athlete, the quiet loner, the social butterfly, or the new kid trying to find their place, I saw everyone as valuable. I made it my mission to find those who seemed overlooked, lonely, or just having a rough day and remind them that they mattered. I wanted people to feel seen, loved, and valued. Whether it was through a kind word, a small act of service, or just my presence, I thrived in creating joy. But bullies? Oh, no ma'am or sir. That was where I drew the line. I couldn't stand to see anyone mistreated. If I caught wind of injustice, you could bet your last dollar that I was going to say something about it. I wasn't about that "sit back and mind your business" life. If there was a wrong, I was determined to make it right. I wrote petitions, rallied for change, and even got a few policies implemented that (believe it or not) are still in effect 25 years later at my high school.

Even then, without realizing it, I was walking in the calling of a servant and a warrior. A protector of people, an advocate for justice, and a fighter for what was right. I was being prepared to stand boldly in faith, to fight the good fight (1 Timothy 6:12), and to be a warrior after God's own heart. They say that whatever personality traits you had before salvation only amplify when you start walking in your purpose. If you were bold in the world, you'll be even bolder in the Kingdom. If you were outspoken, get ready to be a voice for God's people. If you didn't tolerate nonsense before, just wait until you realize how much you really can't tolerate spiritual foolishness. I've heard testimonies of people saying, "I was loud in my sin, so I'll be even louder in my salvation." And let me tell you, God did not put all this fire in me for it to be dimmed now! If I was standing up for people then, you better believe I'll be standing up for God's people now. And that's what this journey is all about. We take the gifts, the personality, the passion, and even the challenges that shaped us and use them to fulfill the divine assignments God has placed in our lives.

So, to anyone reading this who feels like life has just been a whole lot of unnecessary discipline and struggle, know this ... God wastes nothing. Every experience, every lesson, every battle, and even every tear is working together for your good (Romans 8:28).

Trust the process. Stay the course. And when your moment comes to step fully into your purpose.

Late Teen/Young Adult Struggles

So now here come the real-life struggles. I went off to college and was out on my own for the first time ever, removed from the structure and shelter that I had known my entire life. Let's just say that it was a major shock to my system. I made it two years before I ended up coming back home.

I then became a young mother at 21, followed by a failed relationship from my youth. But to God be the glory, it was not a failed co-parenting situation or friendship. Even in the midst of all that, my greatest earthly gift was bestowed upon me, my Jada Boo! Yet, even with such a blessing, I still had to find my identity and joy again … without giving up. It was one of the most challenging stages of my life. To be ripped away from all that I had grown familiar and comfortable with was truly life-changing. I was "green," with no real-life, hard experiences, always expecting the best out of people. My heart for people often led to disappointment, but I was raised to treat others with love, respect, and integrity, always giving them a chance. However, life quickly taught me that kindness is not always reciprocated.

God blessed me with a servant's heart, which often gets taken advantage of and misused. That alone could make anyone want to give up on people, on friendships, and even on love. But for some reason, God didn't equip me to quit. He preserved my ability to love, even when it hurt. He knew that I would need all the bumps and bruises to minister "to the brokenhearted and those crushed in spirit" (Psalm 34:18). He made me built to bend but never to break.

I can give my parents credit for their nurturing and rearing, but all glory belongs to God! Have I been perfect? Absolutely not! I have sinned many, many times and fallen short of the glory of God (Romans 3:23). I knowingly lived outside of His will and, at times, became so entangled in sin that I "forgot" those ways of life were unacceptable to His standards of righteousness and holiness.

But as you mature in Christ and surround yourself with "likeminded people of God" you begin to understand that many of our struggles, aches, and pains stem from our disobedience. In my disobedience, I endured relationships that drained me, distracted me, hurt me and that could have and possibly should have destroyed me physically, mentally, and spiritually. I loved people more than I loved myself, to the point of losing my identity. I tolerated what I knew was unacceptable, pouring out endlessly while receiving little to nothing in return.

I felt shame because I knew better. Not only was I Linda and Garry's daughter, but I am a daughter of the Most High King! I knew I was fearfully and wonderfully made (Psalm 139:14), yet I was living as an option instead of a priority. I had forgotten that I was more precious than rubies and that nothing we desire can compare to the worth that God has placed in us (Proverbs 3:15).

Sin clouds our vision on so many levels. My path wasn't always clear. I took detours. I ignored warning signs. I settled when I shouldn't have. But through it all, God's perfect plan remained intact. All the while, God is patiently waiting for us to obey so He can end the suffering we inflict on ourselves. So many of the trials we endure are unnecessary lessons we could have learned by being in "the Word" and under good leadership instead of walking through the fire on our own. Yet, I thank God that He never took His hand off me, even in my disobedience. Because that's when we give up. That's when the enemy tries to convince us that we are too far gone, too broken, too unworthy to come back. But the devil is a liar and God says otherwise!

He promises, "Surely I am with you always, even to the end of the age" (Matthew 28:20). He reminds us that we can do all things through Christ who strengthens us (Philippians 4:13). He commands us not to grow weary in doing good because, at the right time, we will reap a harvest if we do not give up (Galatians 6:9). And He assures us that the suffering of this present time is not worth comparing with the glory that will be revealed in us (Romans 8:18).

Jesus Himself never gave up. Betrayed, abused, rejected, He pressed on. Even when facing the ultimate sacrifice on the cross He endured because He knew that His suffering had purpose. If we claim to follow Christ then we too must carry that same perseverance in our hearts. We must push forward, trusting that every trial, every heartbreak, and every setback is simply a setup for something greater.

Even when I strayed, even when I didn't fully understand my purpose, God was orchestrating everything to bring me to where I am today. Every lesson, every trial, every closed door, every failed relationship, every broken heart, every disappointment, it was all leading me here. And I'm not done yet. Glory to God!

Accepting "The Assignment" and Never Looking Back!

God has called me to this moment, to this assignment, and to this mission of Kingdom building. And let me tell you I don't take it lightly and certainly don't take it for granted. This isn't just a casual calling or a "maybe if I feel like it" type of deal. No, this is an all-in, burn the bridges, no turning back kind of calling. Because the same God who brought me through the storms before is the same God who will lead me forward into His promises.

Now, if you had asked me years ago if this would be my life, I probably would have laughed … hard. I always knew I was called to help people, to serve, to uplift. But living a life of full-time ministry? Devoting every fiber of my being to God's people, whether it's His children or His leaders? That part? Oh, that caught me off guard. Yet, here I am fully surrendered, fully committed, and fully aware that this is no small assignment. Some days, just as many do, I look at what God has entrusted me with and feel like Moses at the burning bush: "Lord, are You sure You meant to call *me*?" (Exodus 3:11). But God doesn't call the qualified, He qualifies the called. And even when the weight of the assignment feels intimidating and overwhelming, when the responsibility seems too great, I rest in knowing that He who began a good work in me will carry it to completion (Philippians 1:6).

He is positioning me to be a vessel to serve not only the community but my pastor and the people that God will entrust to his ministry and to stand beside the one God has chosen as my Kingdom partner. And that? That is a calling that requires strength, wisdom, humility, grace, discernment and a whole lot of prayer. My purpose is to be a pillar, a source of encouragement, a warrior in the spirit, a servant at heart to uplift, to intercede, to lead by example, and to support the vision that God has placed on my pastor's heart. I aim to be an anchor in the storm, a helpmate in the battle, and a source of unwavering faith when the weight of ministry becomes heavy. This journey is not about titles, it's about servanthood. I'm here because, at the end of the day, ministry is not about accolades or positions; it's about serving with grace, with love, and with an unwavering commitment to God's purpose It's about being clothed in strength and dignity, speaking with wisdom, and watching over the affairs of my household with faithfulness (Proverbs 31:25–27). It's about embracing the responsibility of nurturing, counseling, and guiding others with a heart that mirrors Christ's love.

Now, let's talk about the reality of it all because some people have this fairy-tale idea of ministry life. They think being a pastor or a pastor's wife means sitting pretty in the front row, smiling for the congregation, and hosting glamorous church events. Let me tell you, the oil of anointing comes with crushing, with ridicule and judgment from the people who don't look in the mirror at themselves. The battles that come with this calling are real. The sacrifices? Oh, they're many. But the grace? The grace is more than enough.

I have accepted the fact that a union between a husband and wife, especially one dedicated to Kingdom work, is not just about love songs, date nights, and matching church outfits. It's about a covenant. A divine partnership. It's about understanding that even our love story does not belong to us, it belongs to GOD. Yes, at some point there will be romance, companionship, and joy, but at the core, our purpose is to honor Him and build His Kingdom TOGETHER. Because when two people commit to serving God first, everything else falls into place.

Will the road ahead be easy? Absolutely not. But I refuse to grow weary in doing good because I know that my labor in the Lord is not in vain (1 Corinthians 15:58). No matter what comes—setbacks, trials, or the occasional moment when I feel like throwing in the towel—I will press forward. I will serve. I will love. I will build the Kingdom of God with all that is within me ... AND NEVER GIVE UP!

Because here's the truth—the things that once made me feel like giving up were just stepping stones leading me straight into the arms of purpose. And for that I will forever give God the glory.

To God be the glory for all He has done, for all He is doing, and for all He has yet to do.

And giving up? That's simply not an option. We must TRUST THE PROCESS!

Teka's Acknowledgments

Before I say anything, let me take a moment to honor God! He's my everything, my Savior, my Healer, my Deliverer, my Way-Maker, and my Sustainer. Without Him, I am nothing. With Him, I lack nothing. It is only by His grace that I stand here today, fully aware that every step of my journey has been divinely ordered (Psalm 37:23).

To the people whom God so graciously placed in my life, those who have shaped me, uplifted me, and walked this journey with me, I thank you. No one fulfills their purpose alone and I am beyond blessed to have been surrounded by your love, wisdom, and support every step of the way.

To my auntie, Apostle Dr. Natasha Bibbins, thank you for believing in me and trusting me with your vision to share what thus saith the Lord and to testify of His goodness through my life experiences. Your faith in me has fueled my own and for that I am eternally grateful.

To my incredible parents, Linda and Garry Giddens Sr. You raised me with a foundation so strong that even the fiercest storms of life could not shake it (Matthew 7:24–25). You taught me that family is everything, even to the point where arguing with my siblings was a punishable offense (talk about enforcing unity!). Because of you, I learned resilience, faith, and what it means to stand tall in the face of adversity. Thank you for your love, your sacrifices, and your unwavering belief in the woman God created me to be.

To my siblings, Keta and GL Giddens (Precious we love you too), my built-in best friends. Thank you for always having my back, for the laughter, the memories, and for being my safe place. Life wouldn't be the same without you.

To my beautiful daughter Jada. You are my motivation, my inspiration, and a young woman I deeply admire. Watching you grow into a strong, independent, God-fearing woman who knows her worth has been one of my greatest joys. You are truly one of the reasons I never gave up. Mommy loves you beyond words!

To every spiritual leader, mentor, mother, father, brother, and sister (too many to name) from the past, present, and to come in the future, I am grateful for my village/tribe. No matter how big or small your role was, know that your impact is forever etched into my journey.

To my Saint John Independent Church Family and Friends, "The Church on Fire for God, where the doors swing on the hinges of LOVE." From the moment I walked through those doors you embraced me as one of your own. Your love, support, and encouragement have been a blessing beyond measure and I am honored to walk this journey with you. As our pastor says, "We have not seen nothing yet. The best is yet to come!"

And last, but certainly not least, to my love, my leader, my protector, and my fiancé (as of March 9, 2025—yes, God's timing is impeccable!) Pastor Aaron D. Lewis—thank you for your unwavering love, your guidance, your covering, and your encouragement to *"go forth"* and *"launch out into the deep."* (Luke 5:4). Walking this Kingdom journey with you is a blessing I never saw coming, but God knew exactly what He was doing!

Teka T. Giddens

Teka T. Giddens was born on February 21, 1982, on the beautiful Eastern Shore of Virginia in Northampton County, Sister Teka Giddens was divinely placed into the loving care of her parents, Linda and Garry Giddens Sr. She has three siblings, Precious, Keta, and Garry Jr. (affectionately known as GL) and is a devoted mother to her beautiful daughter, Jada. She also is an aunt to her beloved niece Jaila (Honey Chucky) and nephew Garry III (Rollie).

Teka is a passionate servant of God, a dynamic encourager, and a fierce warrior for the Kingdom. She faithfully serves at Saint John Independent Church under the leadership of Pastor Aaron D. Lewis. With a heart devoted to ministry, she is an active member of the Praise Team, the Usher Board, the Kitchen Committee, and the Women's Ministry, always willing to serve in any capacity wherever God calls her.

Her professional journey has been one of diligence and purpose. With a background in Home Health Office

Management, Human Resources, and Payroll, Teka currently works in Finance for a Community Health Center Network, specializing in Payroll. Even in her career she carries the light of Christ, ensuring that her work is not just a job but a ministry that reflects integrity, excellence, and service as she reminds employees that she assists throughout each day to "Have a great day on purpose."

Whether she is ministering through words, serving her community, or boldly walking in her calling, Teka embodies resilience, unwavering faith, and the undeniable power of divine transformation. She is a living testimony that when God calls, He equips … and when He equips, no weapon formed against her shall prosper (Isaiah 54:17).

Her mission? To uplift, inspire, and remind the world that God is not just the God of yesterday but also the God of right now. And through Him, giving up is never an option.

Contact Information:

FB: GiddensTeka

IG: teka_giddens03

TikTok: tekagiddens2003

Email: tekagiddens1982@gmail.com

Delayed but Not Denied

Peri Hutt

All my years in school I was an honor student who was on the road to success. Not only did I have big hopes and dreams for my future, but so did my parents. If you had asked me in high school what I was going to do afterwards I would have told you that I planned to attend college and major in physical therapy. Once done with college, I wanted to get married and have a family. I was so naïve to think it was that easy. In my young mind, I understood that education was important, and I felt like marriage was the goal, not realizing at the time how difficult life can be with all its ebbs and flows.

Ultimately, I did receive my education, but marriage has not become my reality yet. At the age of 17 my life took an unexpected turn. As I share my story, I pray that it will give someone hope. I want everyone to know that your plan may derail but you can always get back on track as long as you are determined.

I almost gave up on my dreams, but I realized a delay is not a denial.

It Was All a Dream

It was 1995. I was scheduled to graduate from high school in a few short weeks. I was at my senior prom at the Hotel DuPont in Wilmington, DE. I looked stunning in a custom gown that the secretary at my grandmother's job had made for me. Mrs. Anne Braithwaite, I still remember her name. She was masterful with a needle and thread! I showed her a picture from a bridal magazine, and she recreated my dress exactly how it looked in the book. When I went to my final fitting, I almost fainted but dismissed it because I had been running on fumes getting prepared for my big day. I just remember there being so many details. My girlfriend, Kia, was getting her dress made by Mrs. Anne too. Her mother, Mom Bev (as I affectionately called her), took us both up Philly to get our fabric. I decided to go with a goldish champagne color and the top had a lace design and the bottom was satin. It may sound old now with all the beaded gowns, but it was different and classy. I loved it and all the little touches that she added. My girlfriend went with an orange satin with this beautiful iridescent overlay. Our dresses were unique and beautiful.

At the dance, I was prepared and had packed my sanitary napkin in my small purse. I took a break from the dance to use the restroom, but there was nothing. A wave of anxiety flushed over me. I was irregular, but today was supposed to be the day. Thinking back to my lightheadedness now it seemed to all come together and I had a clear picture of what was going on within my body. Now was not the time to go into meltdown mode. I started to panic in my beautiful dress with my beautiful hair and make-up with my French tips. There was nothing I could do that night. Therefore, I gathered myself and rejoined my friends. I forced a smile on my face and went and tried to enjoy the rest of my night. My mind was racing with a swarm of thoughts. I was thinking about college and my parents. My parents probably preoccupied my mind the most because what was I going to do and how was I going to tell them? I knew the news would disappoint them and the rest of my family. It was one month before graduation and my life was over as I knew it to be.

I was glad I was at the dance with a friend versus my boyfriend, now baby daddy at this point. I was more comfortable and knew I would have a better time with him though a few weeks prior I remember asking him if I could take my boyfriend and if he would mind. I wasn't trying to be mean; I was just trying to keep the peace with my then boyfriend. Either way he couldn't go so it worked out. After apologizing profusely, my friend agreed to still go with me. We had a good time, and I was relieved that I went with him afterwards. Since we went to the same school and had the same group of friends it was enjoyable, and I didn't have those awkward moments that sometimes come from bringing someone outside of the school or the friend circle. My date was a gentleman and delivered me home safely. I was home, but my outlook on life was different.

Family History

My parents had invested a lot into me and my education. The timing couldn't have been worse as I was preparing to go to college after high school. I was raised in a two-parent middle-class household in Wilmington, DE. My parents were married, and my father was out of the military by the time I came around. I was definitely an oops baby. My brother and I are exactly a year apart and were born on the same date. I was a week late and my Aunt Leslie always told me I was stubborn. I guess it started in the womb. I was the youngest of four. My mother had my oldest brother and my sister before meeting my father. When they met, after a while they had my brother then me. We were born at the now condemned hospital, Wilmington General. During the '70s most children were born there. Once it was torn down, they built condominiums where the hospital used to stand. They are still there but aren't the same as most things in the city.

I attended People's Settlement for daycare and day camp on the Eastside of Wilmington. My grandmother, Wilda, started the Head Start program there and worked as a social worker. She was my dad's mother and was married to my grandfather, Clarence. My cousin, Karen, was the director for the camp, Rocky Run Day Camp. Both my mother's family and my father's family grew up on the eastside. However, for the most part, we typically resided on the city's north side. My brother, who is a year ahead of me, and I attended Catholic school from first to eighth grades. My mother dropped us off on her way to work at ICI on Concord Pike until we were old enough to walk. I was my brother's shadow, so naturally I was a tomboy. If he wanted to play football in the yard with his friends, that is what I was doing too. I had friends too and we would play games such as hopscotch, jump rope or other games such as red light, green light. Our school colors were brown and yellow. The girls wore a brown plaid dress and once you got to seventh grade, you could then wear a skirt. Most of my classmates I knew from first grade, so we were more like family. By the eighth grade, there were 12 of us and the only boy in my class was my cousin, Cary. I was unprepared when it came to matters of the opposite sex because at that time my parents didn't really talk to you about peer pressure and other challenges I would face as a teenager. They had more of an old-school mindset, and I was pretty much told not to do something "because I said so." I was sheltered to say the least. I entered high school with almost 300 people, and I had a culture shock at first. I learned to navigate, but it was quite an adjustment.

School came naturally to me. I always got good grades, often being on the honor roll, and my parents encouraged me to do well. They stressed the importance of an education. Neither of my parents attended college but still did well. However, they were determined for me to go to school. In seventh grade, I attended a STEM program called FAME. For Delaware, this was where the "smart kids" went. In high school, I also attended a program called Upward Bound. Both programs had opportunities to stay on campus during the summer for a few weeks at the University of Delaware. This was a way to introduce high school students to college life to make the transition smoother. I was the only one of my siblings to attend such programs.

My oldest brother didn't go to college, but he was very good at football and could build anything. He had his first child when I was in seventh grade. My sister had her first baby at 16. Both are very intelligent and could have done anything. My sister is our fashionista and probably missed her calling as a designer or a private investigator because she is a super sleuth. My other brother just wasn't into school. He tried, but school didn't come naturally, so he really had to work at it to get good grades. As such, my parents were a lot more lenient with him than me when it came to school. In 12th grade, he co-opted and was able to go to school and then work with my father who at the time had his own painting business. He learned the skill of painting from father as he had his own painting contracting business. Since he wasn't academically inclined, I think it was important to my father that he had a trade. He is very charismatic and growing up he was my best friend. Because we are so close in age I was basically his shadow. He later joined the Navy after high school. I hated it because it was the first time that we had been separated for a lengthy period of time. When he returned home I was so excited even though we got on each other's nerves. When he returned home, he worked at my family's sneaker store. Therefore, I was the last one and I was supposed to succeed and go to school.

My mother, by trade, worked at a pharmaceutical company doing research and data analysis. Therefore, she would always force me to seek answers for myself when I would ask her something. My parents always kept a set of encyclopedias in the house for that very reason. I know we now have Google, but back in the day you either went to the library to do your research or looked in an encyclopedia. I was naturally curious so I didn't mind when she would tell me to look something up. My father was ex-military and an entrepreneur. He is street smart and has a mind for business. Also, he worked at some of the global chemical companies such as DuPont and Sunolin. When we moved into the Ninth Ward in Wilmington when I was in twelve, it was like we were the Jeffersons, moving on up. My parents made sure we had everything we needed and most of what we wanted. My mother was one of nine and my father was one of seven. They simply did not believe in spoiling children but made sure we were taken care of and had the necessities.

After I graduated from high school, I was enrolled and started at the University of Delaware. I wasn't really showing and still hadn't told my parents. I stayed on campus and I went to class during the week. Considering I was about 20 minutes from home, my parents expected me to come home on the weekends at times. I didn't because I was avoiding them. Sometimes, my boyfriend would come down and spend the weekend with me since my roommate was gone on the weekends because she tutored a child and stayed with the family on the weekends. Everything was going smoothly until I received a call from my mother telling me to come home that following weekend. Little did I know the jig was up; my cousin had told my aunt and my aunt told my mother. Certain calls you don't forget. The amount of fear I had about facing my parents was unexplainable. I went home that following weekend and faced the music. After some unpleasant conversations, I returned to college and my plan was to finish the semester.

However, in November, I started having terrible pains. The pain was not subsiding regardless of what I did. I fearfully called my mom. She, along with my cousin, Darshell, came to the school to pick me up and took me to the hospital. Once I got there, they took me right up to the maternity ward. After a panel of tests, I learned that I had gallstones, and I needed to have my gallbladder removed. I had the surgery and because I was pregnant, I couldn't have the laparoscopic procedure, so I had to have a 12-inch incision to excise the marred organ. My father came to the hospital and brought one of his friends to pray over me and the baby. He was still angry with me, but he didn't want anything to happen to me or my baby.

Once I recovered, I was able to go home. I had to withdraw from my classes and moved out of my dorm and moved back home. The shame I felt was indescribable. *How did I get here? Where did I go wrong?* I did the best I could and tried to heal and prepare for my new baby who would soon be arriving. I had no plan and was clueless as to what I was going to do. My father and I were at odds, as you can imagine, so I tried to spend the least amount of time at home that I could. I would self-exile to my cousin Sharita's house. She had an apartment with her boyfriend and their son in Newark. Also, my boyfriend's mother was excited about the baby, and she didn't mind me staying there. She would even let me borrow her car and gave me a key to their house. My family gave me a baby shower at my Aunt Robin's house. It was simple yet intimate. I loved it and I was very appreciative considering everything.

Life-Changing Moment

On January 29, 1996, I woke my mother up around 2:00 a.m. and told her I thought I needed to go to the hospital. She took me to St. Francis Hospital and later that day, I delivered my daughter, Imani. She was beautiful and looked like a little doll baby. I couldn't believe I had created a person and just kept staring at her and making sure she was breathing while she was sleeping. She was so tiny and I knew that I had to do whatever I needed to in order to care for and protect her. Once I got home and settled, my mother told me I had six weeks to find a job, or my baby and I would need to find somewhere else to go. I didn't know if she was serious or not, but I didn't want to find out. To say that I went into panic mode was an understatement. I found a job in four weeks through a temporary agency working for a company that did process serving and keyed in proxies (paper votes). My grandmother Florence, aka Mom Betty, agreed to watch my child, which gave me some comfort knowing I didn't have to place her into daycare. It wasn't just the expense; it was knowing that she was going to be cared for properly while I was working. I was forever grateful to my grandmother for this extension of love. My cousin, Darshell, had a baby in May of the same year and my grandmother watched her baby too. The following year, my nephew, Armond, was born and he joined the bunch. My great-grandmother Rita, aka Mom Carty, used to have a home-based daycare so I guess it was natural for my grandmother to take on that role for the family. The kids ate good food and were surrounded with love.

Over the next few years, I worked and took care of my child. I got my first car and even returned back to UD. I was commuting and attending school full time while now working at my family's sneaker store as well. Eventually, working and going to school became too much. By now, I had purchased a car and had to pay real bills. I had to choose one and I chose to work so that I could care for my child. I went full time at the store and eventually my daughter's father and I moved in together. I was 19 years old playing house because I thought this was what I was supposed to do. However, moving in together was a mistake. Unfortunately, it wasn't a peaceful exit though. He and I had a discussion and he agreed to move out. I had already spoken with my cousin and she was going to move into my apartment so I didn't have to return home. The night he was supposed to leave, /I went out with my friends and my cousin. We went up Philly and essentially were celebrating my new found freedom...or so I thought. When I returned home it was about 2 a.m. and when I entered the apartment there were candles lit in the bedroom, he was asleep in the bed and the bed was messed up. I was angry. I disrupted his sleep and was yelling because it was obvious, he had someone else in the apartment. I was hurt and I couldn't think straight. I just wanted to leave and he blocked the door. At this point, the situation got physical and I hit him. He grab my arms to avoid me from hitting him. He wouldn't let me just leave. With my hands bond, I couldn't break free so I bit his face. He finally released me and I left the apartment. When I was outside, I was so angry that I kicked the front of his car and his light popped out. I was crying hysterically and got into my car. I drove to a near by phone booth and called home. My mom didn't ask any questions. I guess she could hear it in my voice and she simply said, "Come home!". Just hearing her voice soothed me. I arrived at home and I think she met me at the door. She still didn't ask any questions. I just went to sleep as I finally felt at peace. Things weren't going well for awhile but I was hopeful that things would turn around. As a young girl, you are told how you are supposed to act and you see your parents married. You think you are doing everything right but I never had conversations about how to maintain romantic relationships or how to overcome difficult situations. I knew one thing for sure though, I did not want to be in the relationship with my daughter's father anymore. He did not make me feel good about myself as he consistently talked down on me. After we separated, our relationship was contentious to say the least and he tried to do whatever he could to make my life miserable. I was young and was doing the best I could to keep my head above water.

It wasn't easy but that was the best decision for me and my daughter and I never regretted leaving.

Eventually, I secured a job in banking with the help of my Aunt Leslie. There, I worked and was able to support my daughter and myself. I got my first apartment and upgraded my car. Although I mastered my roles, I was unable to have any sort of upward mobility without a degree. I kept making lateral moves, which didn't do much in terms of my paycheck. I was able to earn bonuses, which motivated me to do well, but my hours weren't great working in a call center. I opted for steadier hours and took up a part-time job since most times my daughter went to her grandmothers on the weekend. That allowed me to be home during the week, especially with her being in school. I even enrolled in a first-time homebuyer's program but soon realized I was not going to be able to afford a home on my current salary. I wasn't a stranger to hard work as I often worked multiple jobs to support my daughter and I. I took the money I was saving for my house and enrolled in school at Delaware Technical and Community College.

A Second Chance

I was attending school when I met a guy. He seemed to be everything that I was looking for. He was kind and sort of quiet and a low-key good guy. I was 29 at the time and became pregnant with my second child. Prior to our daughter arriving, we moved in together. He and his family treated my older daughter as a part of theirs and he provided for her as he did our own child. Life was good. Our daughter was born on October 14, 2007. Londyn had arrived and she was the spitting image of her father. Imani was an awesome big sister and was protective of her little sister. My boyfriend and I were happy. My grandmother agreed to watch Londyn and said she would be her last child since she was now in her seventies. According to her that was her baby. She loved Londyn and said she kept her young. I thought I had finally gotten things right and that things were back on track. He and I talked and agreed that once our daughter was almost two it was time for me to return to school. At that time, we both had new jobs. We both started them right before our daughter was born. I was quickly becoming a rising star at my new company, and I did what I needed to do to gain exposure and learn as much as I could. I had moved into a new department on a temporary basis, which had the potential to be a career. This made me even more determined to complete my degree.

My educational journey started as part-time but had grown into full-time classes. To earn an undergrad degree, you needed 120 credit hours. Each class was typically three credit hours, which means essentially you had to complete 40 classes to get a degree. A part-time schedule would have taken too long. Therefore, I started taking on a full caseload and was managing four to five classes a semester. I took advantage of hybrid classes and everything in between. I tried to take as many online classes as I could to minimize my time outside of the home. Regardless, my home life suffered. Working full time and going to school full time didn't allow me to be the most present girlfriend or mother. I wasn't running the streets, but my absence was noticed.

Eventually we moved into a house and a year later our relationship ended. I was heartbroken and immediately felt like I did something wrong. However, I wasn't unfaithful and I was very trusting. Even before I was in school, I didn't badger him about too much. He came home every night and he assisted in raising both of my girls. He worked shift work and sometimes he would be tired but he still did what he needed to do. I thought this is what family and relationships were about, building something so the family could be in a better position. I took the break-up personal and struggled with my feelings and emotions. I went from a team of two to a team of one and life was different now in terms of my every day life. I allowed my pain and hurt to fuel me to do better. The following year, I graduated with my degree and purchased my first home. I was back in school to earn my Paralegal Certification, which I completed on the heels on my undergrad degree. Although we were no longer together, my daughter's father was still supportive and helped with keeping the girls while I finished school when necessary. We co-parent well and are still friends. My mother, his mother and other friends and family helped as well. It was truly a team effort as it does take a village.

Starting Over

The Bible tells us in Romans 3:23 that we all fall short of the glory of God. I was no exception. I wanted better, I prayed and still do daily. I pray for anything from strength to healing to discernment. I would be delusional if I portrayed that I alone made it through this thing called life. God guided me every step of the way. There were times when I was frustrated and threw up my hands and there were times when I just broke down and told Him how thankful I was. Either way, whether I was up or I was down, I knew that I was never alone

In the past few years, I was promoted to a vice president within my department, I am the board member of a non-profit organization, and I have become a pillar within my organization. Also, I always wanted to join sorority. However, because of my non-traditional education journey, I thought that was something I wouldn't be able to achieve. However, in March 2022, I was inducted into the best sorority for me! My kids are thriving and finding their way and I am in a position to do things differently. I have received various awards and accolades and, aside from my children, the thing that brings me joy is to see my dad post something on social media bragging about me. Also, when I see an old family friend and they tell me my dad or my mom or someone else in my family said they are proud of me. If you knew all I went through you would understand why I am appreciative. My life's experiences have humbled me. There is much more to this story, but at the end of the day it all happened with the grace of God! I owe it all to Him because without Him, I am nothing.

My Boaz has not found me yet, but I remain hopeful. I am enjoying life and am experiencing new things with friends or solo. I am in a place where I enjoy my own company. . I have three grandchildren, and they are the light of my life. I am present for them and my children. I love to travel and spend time with friends and family. I do work within the community, which is fulfilling and gives me purpose. I am thankful for my journey and still believe a delay is not a denial.

Peri's Acknowledgements

I would like to acknowledge my parents, Craig and Carmella Hutt. I appreciate that each time I fell down, you were right there to pick me up and to point me in the right direction. Thank you for never abandoning me even when I made some questionable decisions. I appreciate our "no judgment" zone as an adult and love you for the way that you love me. Thanks for your support and, although my journey started rough, I hope I have made you both proud.

To my children, Imani and Londyn, thank you for being my children. You are both a blessing and drive and challenge me in various ways. Thanks for keeping me on my toes and for pushing me to be greater!

To my friends and family ... there are too many to name. Thank you for your place in my life. You each know you are near and dear to me and keep me sane on a daily basis either with a funny meme or a welcoming smile when we connect. Thank you!

To Dr. Natasha Bibbins and Mrs. Carla Manuel, thank you for extending the invitation for this project to me and for your patience. I am truly appreciative and humbled by this experience.

Last, but certainly not least, thank you to my Lord and Savior for continuing to keep me even when I fell short ... but God!

Peri Hutt

Peri Hutt currently resides in Wilmington, DE and is a professional with over 20 years of experience in the banking industry. She is the proud mother of two daughters, Imani and Londyn, and three grandchildren, Sawyer, Tristan and Willow. She has served on the board of a non-profit organization for almost 10 years. She is a proud member of Sigma Gamma Rho Sorority, Inc. where she serves as the chair for the local programs of her chapter, Delta Tau Sigma, in Dover, DE. Peri has taken on several leadership roles within her organization and currently serves as the co-chair for the Black Professionals Resource Group.

In her spare time, she enjoys spending time with her family. She is close with her mother, Carmella, and father, Craig, and she has four brothers and two sisters. She has a close-knit relationship with her family and loves to attend family gatherings. She has a large family and is said to have over

100 cousins as her father is one of seven and her mother is one of nine.

She loves attending shows or hanging with her best friend, Tara, or her PPP Possee. Also, she enjoys traveling with her cousins on their annual vacations. Peri is a huge proponent of living life and doing it big because you only get one life to live. You may see her post a reel on her social media page about her most recent journey or a party she attended!

Peri Hutt

302-494-4409

IG @Partygirl302

THE EDGE OF GIVING UP IS WHERE BREAKTHROUGHS BEGIN

Dr. Natasha Bibbins

There's a saying that goes, "When you're going through some rough times, keep going." At times, that's all we can do: keep moving forward, even when the path ahead seems impossible and the weight of our struggles feels too much to bear. I've been there, standing on the edge of giving up, questioning whether I had the strength to keep fighting. In those moments, it seemed easier to walk away, to let go of the dreams and goals I had worked so hard for. But little did I know, it was in those very moments of doubt and despair that something extraordinary was about to unfold.

In my chapter is the story of my journey from the brink of surrender to the unexpected triumphs that followed. It's a story of resilience, of fighting through the darkness when all you see is the endless road ahead. The truth is I almost gave up more times than I care to admit. But who would have thought that just beyond that breaking point, there was a turning point—a moment that would change everything. Through each challenge, I learned lessons about strength, perseverance, and the incredible power of holding on just a little longer. If you're reading this, it's likely that you, too, have faced your own doubts, your own moments of wanting to give up. This book is for you—to remind you that the greatest victories often lie just beyond the moments when we almost let go.

Running from My Problems, or So I Thought

There's a strange sense of relief that comes with running away from your problems. It feels like freedom, a fleeting moment where you convince yourself that out of sight truly means out of mind. I told myself that leaving my troubles behind was the best solution. New places and fresh starts sounded enticing, almost romantic. Surely, if I put enough distance between myself and my issues, they'd shrink into insignificance, maybe even vanish altogether. What I didn't realize was that the baggage I carried wasn't just physical; it was emotional, invisible, and tied tightly to me, no matter where I went.

At first, the distraction worked. New surroundings gave me plenty to focus on—finding my way around, meeting new people, and adjusting to unfamiliar routines. But it didn't take long for the cracks to show. The problems I thought I'd left behind had a way of creeping back in, no matter how fast or far I ran. It wasn't the environment I'd been trying to escape; it was my unresolved feelings, fears, and mistakes. The newness wore off and I found myself staring down at the same issues, now magnified by the loneliness of being in a strange place.

The hardest realization was understanding that running wasn't solving anything, it was only delaying the inevitable. Problems don't disappear just because you avoid them. They fester, growing roots in your mind until they seem larger and more intimidating. Facing them felt terrifying, but I started to see that confronting my fears was the only way to loosen their grip. It required honesty, acknowledging my role in the situation, and embracing the discomfort of vulnerability. With time, I began to feel lighter, not because I'd run farther but because I'd stopped running altogether.

It was not long before I realized that running from "my home" was not helping me. To be honest, running made me tired, stressed, and I missed a part of me. I thought that my leaving would push me to happiness; it actually made matters worse. What I learned through this experience is that peace doesn't come from avoidance but from resolution. Running away might offer temporary relief, but it's never a permanent fix. Healing comes from turning inward, addressing what's broken, and building resilience to handle the challenges life throws at us. The act of standing still and facing our pain head-on is what gives us the strength to move forward, not as someone running from their problems but as someone ready to overcome them.

I understood what I needed to do, so I planned to leave Michigan and head back to Virginia after my daughter graduated from high school. For once, I was ready to stop running and face my problem. You see, no one really knew how bad my life was before I decided to leave. You can say that I wore it well, smiling outwardly while dying on the inside. I kept asking myself, "Is going back the right decision?" I was reminded of the scripture where Jesus had delivered the demon-possessed man and he wanted to go with Jesus, but Jesus said to him in Luke 8:39, *"No, go back to your family, and tell them everything God has done for you."* It was at that point that I knew I had to face the demons of my past.

Standing Face-to-Face with ME (The Man in the Mirror)

There's something both unsettling and liberating about looking into the mirror and truly seeing yourself, not just your reflection, but the person behind the eyes: the flaws, the fears, the dreams, and the doubts. For years, I avoided that kind of confrontation, glossing over the truth of who I was. The man in the mirror felt like a stranger, someone I didn't want to know too deeply. It was easier to focus on surface-level details, to keep moving through life without questioning the choices that brought me here or the parts of myself I tried to hide.

But one day, I couldn't look away. I found myself standing face-to-face with the man in the mirror, unable to ignore the weight of my gaze. There was no hiding anymore. In that moment, I saw the person I had become, not just the good but also the parts I didn't want to acknowledge. I saw the regrets I tried to bury, the mistakes I was too ashamed to admit, and the potential I had been too afraid to pursue. The mirror didn't lie, and for the first time, I realized that honesty with myself was the only path forward.

That confrontation wasn't easy. It felt like stripping away years of denial, standing bare before someone I had long avoided. The man in the mirror didn't judge me, but he also didn't let me off the hook. He demanded accountability, not perfection. He asked me to own my story, to take responsibility for the choices that shaped my life, and to forgive myself for the times I fell short. Through that process, I began to understand that growth isn't about never making mistakes; it's about learning from them and daring to do better.

Standing face-to-face with the man in the mirror changed everything. It gave me the courage to embrace my imperfections and the strength to work on the parts of me that needed healing. I no longer fear what I see when I look in the mirror because I know the reflection staring back at me is someone I can trust, someone I'm proud to have become. The mirror became less of a critic and more of a companion, a reminder that self-awareness is the foundation of self-love. In the end, the man in the mirror wasn't my enemy—he was my greatest teacher.

The Mirror Showed Me Something

It was an ordinary morning, or so I thought. The sunlight streamed through my window, painting golden streaks across my room. I rolled out of bed, groggy and uninterested in anything. As I shuffled to the bathroom, something strange caught my eye. At first, I thought it was just my tired eyes playing tricks on me because of my lack of sleep. But as I leaned closer, I realized the reflection wasn't quite right. My own face seemed unfamiliar, not just in the usual "I need more sleep" way, but sharper somehow, with eyes that glimmered like they knew a secret I didn't.

For some reason, the mirror started responding to me and "told me about myself while staring at me." As I kept staring in the mirror, I realized that I hated my own reflection. I went back to bed and lay down. This hurts because I remember this like it was yesterday. With tears in my eyes, I reached for my journal and began to write. What I was writing at that time may shock some people because what I was writing was a letter to my children. I always pride myself on being a great mother to my children; I would move mountains if necessary to get them what they needed. So, why was my mirror showing me that I was a failure? Although the mirror made me look like a failure, mirrors don't reflect my worth. Sometimes, our minds can trick us into believing we're failures, but that's not the truth of who we are.

Everyone goes through tough moments and facing setbacks doesn't define us. So, why was I having trouble shaking off the failure in the mirror? It was so bad that I felt like suicide was the answer. In my journal, I wrote that I felt like my children would live a better life without me. Who would have thought that I would allow the enemy to get into my mind and make me feel like I was nobody? Suicide felt like the answer because it seemed like the only way that I would find relief and escape my unbearable pain, because of my overwhelming life circumstances. Here's the twist: who would have thought that it would be my child that the Lord would use to stand up in front of the church and ask for prayer for his mother? But get this: he asked for prayer at the same time I was trying to commit suicide. God used my son to interrupt the service and say, "Pray for my mommy!" When God has a plan for your life, the enemy will do anything he can to stop you from reaching your destiny.

Who Would Have Thought?

Who would have thought that a person who had attempted to take their own life would be the same person that God would use to encourage others to live? I am "she." I am the same person whose heart is devoted to uplifting others through the powerful message of God's love and grace. With every word that I speak, I am constantly reminding those around me that they are never alone, no matter how challenging life may get. It's my faith that shines through in every conversation, offering encouragement drawn from scripture that reassures others of God's promises. Whether in moments of joy or sorrow, God has anointed me to have a unique ability to bring peace and hope, showing others that God's Word can be a source of strength and comfort in all circumstances. 2 Chronicles 15:7 says, "*but as for you, be strong and do not give up, for your work will be rewarded.*"

I believe in the power of God. I know that He changed me into His likeness. My life is not my own; I have been bought with a price that I can never repay.

In 1 Corinthians 6:30, the Amplified version of the Bible says, "*You were bought with a price, [you were actually purchased with the precious blood of Jesus and made of His own]. So then, honor and glorify God with your body.*"

So, the next time you start feeling like you want to give up, remember that giving up is not an option. Ask God to help you and ask Him to point you to great company.

The devil had a plan, and that plan was to destroy me so I could not do the work of my Father, who gave me life. If you do not get anything else from this story, remember that God gave your life, and He is the only one who should take it. God loves you so much that He has already planned your life for you—all you have to do is be obedient and walk into the victory that God has given you. What if I had given up? That's right; you would not be reading my story!

Let's Pray:

Father God, thank you for using me to be an example for others to follow. I thank You, Lord, for allowing me to speak Your Word to those near and far. May my actions continue to reflect the compassion and kindness that I preach about. Through unwavering faith, I will teach others that no struggle is too big for God and that nothing can keep us away from His love. Who would have thought that a mistake was a way for us to learn about your saving grace? Who would have thought that, through our devotions and prayers, your love was covering a multitude of sins? Who would have thought that the beginning of fear (reverence) was the beginning of wisdom? God, I thank you for never giving up on me. Thank you and I know my best days are ahead of me. As Romans 8:18 says, *"For I reckon that the sufferings of this present time are not worthy to be compared with the glory which shall be revealed in us."* Teach me to be patient, in Jesus' Mighty Name.

Amen!

Natasha's Acknowledgements:

I would like to first thank God for all He has done in my life. This is not a cliché because when I think about all the things God has done for me, all the ways He made for me, all the things He protected me from, I can only thank Him. I thank my husband and my best friend, Mr. Michael Bibbins, for your patience, support, and unselfish love throughout this journey. Thank you for always encouraging me to be better. Your famous words to me are always, "Be the best version of you," and I am truly GRATEFUL that God allowed you to be my husband. The Bible says in Proverbs 18:22 (KJV), *"Whoso findeth a wife findeth a good thing, and obtaineth favour from the Lord."* I thank God for choosing me to be your FAVOR!

I want to thank my children, William and Wilniqua Battle, who have always been the reason why I strive to overcome all barriers every day. I want to thank my family and friends for their love and support. Lastly, I would like to thank every person who has supported my ministries through the years. You all will never know how much it means to me to have you in my life. I remember a trusted voice said, *"A leader without any followers would be a **woman** taking a lonely walk."* Thank you all for not allowing me to walk alone. I love you all!

Dr. Natasha Bibbins

Natasha Bibbins is a God-fearing woman who loves the Lord and her family. She is a Wife, Mother, Prophet, Pastor, Coauthor, Author, Certified Life and Executive Leadership Coach, Sister, and Friend. She is the Founder of Natasha Bibbins Ministries, Forever Fire Empowerment (501c3), Sisters Empowering Sisters Ministries, The ReCharge Movement (501c3), and Recharge Outreach Ministry.

She is the visionary of the Walker Family Prayer Call. She believes in the principle that family is her first ministry, as spoken in 1 Timothy 3:5: *"If anyone does not know how to manage his own family, how can he take care of God's church?"*

Natasha also became a best-selling coauthor in 2020 for the book *Dreamer on the Rise*, compiled by Dr. Kishma George, and again in 2022 for the book *Called to Intercede*. She is also the author of *Recharge Empowerment and Journal*, *God Will Right Your Wrong*, and an Amazon Best-Selling Author for God Will Right Your Wrong Too, with some amazing co-authors!

Natasha received an honorary Doctor of Christian Leadership degree from the School of the Great Commission Theological

Seminary in January 2021, while pursuing her Ph.D. in Strategic Leadership at Liberty University.

Professionally, Natasha has a master's degree in management, a bachelor's degree in business management, an associate degree in business administration, and a second master's degree in public administration.

In 2022, she was honored with two awards: a Servant Leader Award and a Walking in Grace Leadership Award.

She is married to Minister Michael Bibbins and is blessed to have two children, Wilniqua and William, three "bonus" children, and one granddaughter.

Natasha's favorite scripture is Romans 8:18: *"For I reckon that the sufferings of this present time are not worthy to be compared to the glory which shall be revealed in us."* This scripture reminds her to keep pressing and keep pushing because greatness is right around the corner.

Dr. Natasha Bibbins

Contact Information:

Facebook: DrNatasha Bibbins

Instagram: DrNatasha Bibbins

Clubhouse: DrNatasha Bibbins

YouTube: DrNatasha Bibbins

Website: www.natashabibbins.com

Email: admin@natashabbins.com

Recharge Outreach Ministry Phone: 757-652-2245

www.ingramcontent.com/pod-product-compliance
Lightning Source LLC
Chambersburg PA
CBHW071209160426
43196CB00011B/2240